Editors
Tracy Loffer, M. Ed.
Ermily R. Smith, M.A. Ed.

Editorial Project Manager
Elizabeth Morris, Ph.D.

Editor-in-Chief
Sharon Coan, M.S. Ed.

Cover Artist
Brenda DiAntonis

Art Coordinator
Kevin Barnes

Imaging
Alfred Lau

Product Manager
Phil Garcia

Publisher
Mary D. Smith, M.S. Ed.

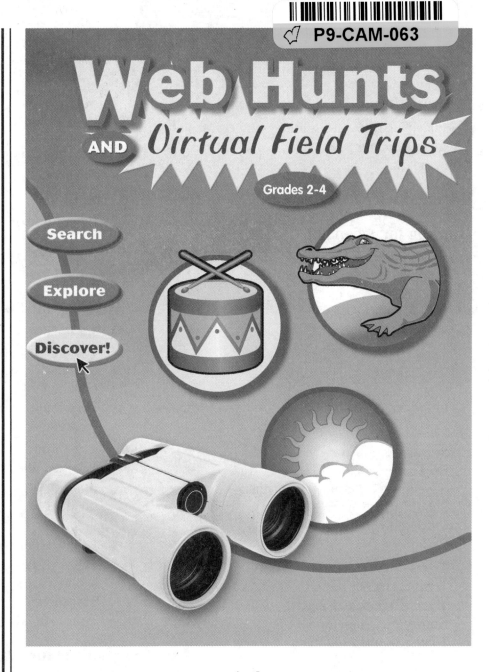

Web Hunts AND *Virtual Field Trips*

Grades 2-4

Search

Explore

Discover!

Author

Caryn Dingman

Teacher Created Resources

Teacher Created Resources, Inc.
6421 Industry Way
Westminster, CA 92683
www.teachercreated.com
ISBN 13: 978-0-7439-3812-9
©2002 Teacher Created Resources, Inc.
Reprinted, 2007
Made in U.S.A.

Table of Contents

Table of Contents (cont.)

Hunting for Language Arts

Introduction to Virtual Field Trips

Trips Across America

Trips to the Animal Kingdom

Trips Around the World

Appendix

About This Book

Why Use a Scavenger Hunt or Virtual Field Trip?

The purpose of a scavenger hunt is to follow directions while visiting different places and collecting certain items. The students visit Web sites, read information, answer specific questions, and then use their new knowledge in unique and interesting ways. Hunts and trips help to advance valuable skills, including research, information management, and technological skills.

When our curriculum was recently re-written to align with state standards adopted by our state's Department of Education, I was left with several problems. Our current textbooks did not support some of the new information we were expected to cover. Our district curriculum guide is very specific in regard to the length of time allotted to each content area per week. In addition, our new state standards for science and technology expected technology integration in all subjects.

To address these issues, I began scouring the Internet for sites suitable to use with primary students. Although standards may vary from district to district and state to state, similarities are quite marked. Some of the hunts and trips may be used as stand-alone activities, designed to teach about a topic or concept with follow-up discussion. Most are meant to be used in conjunction with resources that are already available to you—other Internet sites, current textbooks, library resources, videos, etc.

Each hunt or trip will list student learning objectives, background information detailing pre- and post-lesson activities, and other Internet resources. Other resources, such as books or videos, may be available to you in your school libraries. If these additional resources are not readily available, you may want to recommend these items for purchase by your school district.

Lesson Objectives

The following student learning objectives apply to all the lessons in this book:

- The student will be able to read critically in all content areas.
- The student will be able to learn to read independently.
- The student will be able to read and respond to non-fiction.
- The student will be able to utilize a Web browser and do an online search to answer age-appropriate questions.

Specific learning objectives for individual lessons are located on each Teacher page.

About the Internet Sites Listed in this Book

Each of the activities in this book has at least one suggested Internet site, though there are many others that could be used to complete the activity. At the time this book was printed, all sites were operational, but the Internet changes constantly, and some sites may not work when you or your students attempt to access them at a later date.

Therefore, on each page, the URL of a search engine such as Google.com has also been added with suggested keywords. If the suggested site does not work, you can go to your favorite search engine and type the keywords to search for another site to use. (See What to Do if a Web Site Address Doesn't Work on page 5 for additional tips on troubleshooting.)

About This Book *(cont.)*

What to do if a Web Site Address Doesn't Work

- Check to make sure you typed the address EXACTLY as it appears, with all the characters (such as _, ~, //, etc.).
- Click the Refresh button at the top of your screen
- Enter the address again
- Type only the address of the home page and navigate from there. For example, if the address

http://www.teachercreated.com/cgi-bin/urlsearch.cgi?2187 doesn't work, try truncating it to become: **http://www.teachercreated.com**. Then, click the links on the home page to find the specific Web page you are looking for. In some cases, the Web site will have a search engine in which you can type a keyword and find what you are looking for.

Note: Web sites and Web pages are different things. A Web site usually consists of multiple Web pages, with a home page and several pages linked to the home page viewable by clicking buttons on the home page. A Web page is a single page, such as a home page or a linked page.

Grade Level Adaptations

The activities within this book are designed for primary students. When you read through an activity that seems to be either too young or too old for your learners, you are encouraged to make modifications. When making activities more appropriate for younger students, cut down on the number of objectives and focus on one or two that are the most appropriate. Similarly, when advancing an activity, try to incorporate additional objectives that support your classroom learning in the same area of study. Creating a simpler or more complex version of the student activity page can alter many of the activities within this book. Try to focus on the parts of the existing activities that your learners can do, rather than on the parts they cannot do.

Classroom Management Suggestions

I am fortunate to have five computers available for students' use in my classroom, as well as a computer lab containing 16 machines. When I first began using the hunts and trips in my classroom, I did not attempt to have more than five students working on the Internet at a time. The initial questions from just five students were enough to keep me moving from machine to machine for the entire fifteen-minute session. As children gained comfort and confidence in using the technology, I was able to have more students working on the Internet at one time, often completing a hunt in the computer lab.

My 90-minute science block, two or three afternoons a week, allowed five groups with five students each to rotate through the computer center. The rest of my class has independent work assignments, allowing my attention to remain focused on children working on the computers.

Final Note

The younger your students are, the less likely they are afflicted with the dreaded "If I touch this computer key I will: delete everything or destroy the computer" disease. Most children are perfectly willing to take risks in learning how to use technology. Much of what I have learned has been from observing my own students. They have inspired me and always remind me that I am a learner as well as a teacher.

Online Research

Online research is an inexact art form rather than a precise science. When we consider the multitude of information available through the Internet, we must also consider the ramifications of such a collection on student research.

There are several schools of thought when considering online research for students. Of course, much of the reasoning depends on the age and ability levels of the students. Though each individual situation should be considered, it is most common for schools to feel safest with a standard response or position. Let's take a look at the prevailing attitudes about online research for elementary students.

Willy-Nilly: Some teachers allow their students to go online to do research without any parameters at all. Sadly, this policy is usually a result of the teacher's lack of knowledge, rather than a conscious approach to online research. These teachers often rely on the knowledge levels of their students, often greater than their own, to make the decisions for them. Though many teachers wind up with this kind of Internet use, many others create this method purposefully. They view open use of the Internet as a positive thing. They recognize the fact that Internet use has permeated our society, and they want their students to be well versed in its use without restrictions. These students are growing up in a world where they have access to the Internet almost everywhere.

Don't Go Near It: Other teachers and schools think that because of the vast amount of information that is "out there," it is developmentally inappropriate for elementary students to use any kind of search engine or tool. Teachers in this camp think that it is their job to provide the students with a safe arena for their searches. As such, these teachers usually provide their students with small collections of three to six Web sites to use for each specific activity on which they're working. Generally, these teachers are not impressed with the hit-or-miss method of researching through search engines. They think that it teaches better research skills when they provide the specific documents—documents they know contain the information the students need, documents they know to be accurate, documents which support rather than detract from the learning objectives.

In Between: There is, as exists for most situations in life, a happy middle ground—an in-between that borrows from each end of the spectrum to create another choice. Many teachers find themselves operating in this middle ground. With some activities, these teachers might provide specific Web sites to be used, while with other projects they may allow their students to use kid-friendly search engines in order to train them.

These teachers know that if the intent of going online is to collect information, their students should each have, at the bare minimum, a piece of paper and a pencil in hand when they do so. Even better, they know that their students need to have an activity specific note-taking exercise of some kind. We've provided you with an Internet Research Road Map (Appendix—page 142), which is designed to help students be more purposeful in their use of the Internet. These note-taking forms will help students to use their time more wisely.

Online Research *(cont.)*

In Between *(cont.)*: Teachers in this middle ground also know that their students need to be trained in the use of search engines. Since many of the engines have numerous links, advertising, and extraneous information, it's very easy for students (especially those who are easily distracted) to be drawn away from their purpose. Students need to be shown what to ignore and what to focus on while they're researching. They need to know how to properly word an Internet search, a skill which baffles many adults, let alone elementary students. They need to have an understanding of the organization of the results that the search engines return. All of these needs can be met through simple practice. These teachers usually choose one or two kid-friendly engines to explore with their students, helping them become acclimated to the Internet environment.

Kid-friendly Search Engines

There are a variety of search engines that are designed for school-aged children. Each one of these engines has specific details that you'll need to know about before taking children to them. We recommend that you go to these sites and literally play around on them. Do some searches of topics you're likely to ask your children to do. Get a feel for the return results. Look for organization and readability levels of the site. You know your learners best, so you'll be the best judge of which kiddie engines to use. The most important thing is that you feel comfortable with the process before taking your learners to it.

You might want to employ a few classroom procedures when using the search engines. Try these on for size:

- Have your students write their searching words on index cards and make sure they show them to you so that you can give them guidance and direction before they go online.

- Make a class rule that everyone pays attention to only the top three or four results. This can come in handy when the search engine brings back a list of hundreds!

- When you're first starting out, ask students to answer this question: How could I have made my search stronger? Keep a running list of answers on a poster in the room so that others can improve their skills too!

- Establish search partnerships that allow students to go online in pairs so that they can have two sets of eyes and two brains involved in their searching!

Internet Safety

Certainly one of the main concerns of the "online teacher" is Internet safety. By this point in time, most school systems have created some provision, policy, or statement of philosophy regarding student use of the Internet. Fueled by concerns from parents and occasional bad press, Internet use has gotten a bad rap in some areas. We'd like to address the issue of Internet safety in hopes of providing some guidance to teachers who might be just starting out and affirmation to those who have been traveling the information superhighway safely for years. Teachers should always provide both a purposeful use and appropriate supervision to their online activities.

Purposeful Use

How is the Internet approached in your classroom? Is it treated as a toy or a tool? There is a dangerous message being sent in classrooms where children are rewarded for completed work and good behavior with extra time to "play" on the Internet. In classrooms where the Internet is treated like the powerful tool that it is, there is a greater likelihood that the Internet will be used appropriately. The core of this debate about approaches is summed up in one little word: *intent*.

How is the Internet used in your classroom? When you ask your learners to go online to find something about whales, you're setting them up for a frustrating experience. They might find something, they might not. We wouldn't dream of standing a fourth grader at the doors to the New York Public Library and shoving him gently into the abyss, saying to him, "Run in there and discover something about whales." We'd go with him, guide him through the card catalog, bring him to the section on animals, point out the shelves where the whale books are located, and help them find five books which might give him good information. We should treat the Internet the same way by telling our students to go to a class bookmarks page (a Web site collection of teacher-approved, content-specific sites) to find five facts about whales that we instruct them to write down on index cards. Then we've set them up for success!

Beyond the intent behind our use of the Internet is another word which comes in handy in this discussion: *direction*. It is imperative that we give our students a specific direction when they go online. They should go to some specific place and should do some specific thing when they get there. As we discussed in the section on online research, there is just too much information out there for students to manage alone. It is developmentally inappropriate to expect third, fourth, and fifth graders to be able to manage search results in excess of even 50 hits, let alone searches that bring back thousands of hits. Send your young students to a specific site or collection of sites that you've already approved. Be sure that they know they're expected to do something specific once they get there. Empower them with pre-printed Internet index cards. On one side print the word "Target" where they can write the URL or page name of the Web site they're going to. On the other side, print "Action" where they can write down what action they have to take once they have arrived at the site and read the content.

Internet Safety (cont.)

Appropriate Supervision

The second Golden Rule of Internet safety is providing appropriate supervision. Much of this will depend on your school's philosophy about Internet use. Most schools have a requirement that students have some kind of supervision while they're online. That supervision might be peer supervision or adult supervision. Adult supervision allows for greater accountability.

Of course, age also plays a part here. We have different concerns about Internet safety when working with high school students than we do when working with elementary students. The adult supervision for elementary school students often has more to do with helping them with the technology than it does with protecting them from harm's way. The location of the computers has a lot to do with providing supervision. If the computers are in your classroom, then you have greater control of the situation. Make sure the computers are positioned so that you can see the screens from anywhere in the room. If the computers are located elsewhere, in a lab or in the media center, then make arrangements to have a staff member from the media center or a parent volunteer provide supervision.

Class Expectations

When considering Internet safety, it's important to make sure that we recognize the importance of having clear expectations of our students regarding their use of the Internet. Let them know what kind of task commitment you require, what kind of behavior is appropriate, and what the consequences are if they don't meet those expectations. Most schools or school systems require students to sign an Acceptable Use Policy (AUP) that outlines appropriate use of the Internet. One thing to consider with an AUP is that you want to make sure that it is written on a level the students can understand, rather than in legalese which amounts to a signature without understanding. We've included a copy of an elementary-level AUP in the Appendix (page 140).

Time Constraints

One of the best strategies to use when you're attempting to ensure Internet safety is to place time constraints on your students' use of the Internet. If they know they have a limited amount of time to go online, they're more likely to use that time to accomplish their goals. Time constraints are often a naturally occurring factor because of the ratio of students to computers, so this is a strategy that can be employed without much effort.

Filtering Software

Many school systems are using filtering software to help protect their children. The most important thing to consider here is that we should not allow the presence of a filtering program to lull us into a false sense of security. Filters or not, we should employ other safety strategies.

The bottom line with Internet Safety is this: If your students are trained to treat the Internet as a powerful tool, if they are supervised in their use, if they have specific purposes and objectives when they're online, and if they have a limited amount of time to be online, their online safety is much more secure.

Introduction to Web Hunts

On the following pages you will find hunts that span a variety of topics from math to social studies. Each of the hunts has a key question or focus point that helps your students stay focused on their topic.

Key Questions and Statements

Hunting for Science

What are the names and characteristics of the four seasons?

How can the five senses be used to describe the seasons?

Write a haiku about a season.

How is weather the same or different in two separate locations?

What different types of waves does sound make?

What attributes of musical instruments are the same and which are different?

What type of invention could prevent sound from escaping?

What careers are available in the music industry?

What are the characteristics and habitats of wild Asian tigers?

What other fish and reptiles are named after the tiger?

What is the same and what is different about the tiger and one of its namesakes?

What are the types and properties of matter?

How can similes be used to compare and describe objects?

How can can I decide if matter is a solid or a liquid?

What types of renewable energy are available?

What forces are involved in creating soil?

How are fossils formed?

What are the phases of the moon?

How can a graph be used to show the phases of the moon for specific dates?

Create a poem about the moon.

Hunting for Social Studies

What activities happen on farms and why is farming important?

Write an animal story using a published story as a model.

What is life like for students in another country?

How is your life the same and how is it different from a student in another country?

Why are folk tales similar in different cultures?

What are some ways to communicate with students in another country?

Key Questions and Statements (cont.)

Hunting for Social Studies (cont.)

What statistics are available for your town and other cities in the United States?

How can a friendly letter be organized?

How can information about a family be organized?

What is the most common birthplace of the class' family members?

What was the most common mode of transportation to school in the past?

How are life experiences the same and how are they different for older and younger family members?

Hunting for Math

What can be discovered about geometric shapes?

Read and illustrate a story about the tangram.

How can tangram shapes be arranged to make a picture?

What place values can numbers have?

How does a number change when its place or position changes?

What numbers and pictures help identify the value of money?

How can money be added together to buy an item?

What important pictures and words appear on a coin?

How many items can be purchased with a specific amount of money?

How can a money story be planned?

What is the history of clocks and why do people have them?

What shapes, patterns, and figures can be used on a clock?

Hunting for Language Arts

Which beginning and ending consonants join together to make words?

Create a short tale with words and pictures from the Internet.

What is an acrostic poem?

How can one word be used to create a poem?

What important information can be discovered about Paula Danziger?

What important information can be discovered about Laura Numeroff?

What important information can be discovered about Elvira Woodruff?

What important information can be discovered about Jane Yolen?

Seasons

Background

The passing of the seasons brings about many changes in all things around us. This hunt will allow students to explore the reasons for seasonal changes and will help them understand that seasons refer to groupings of different months making up particular parts of the year.

Objectives

The student will be able to identify seasonal changes and why they occur.

The student will be able to identify the months during each season.

The student will be able to use the five senses to describe the seasons.

The Hunt

Activity One: The Reasons for the Seasons

Key Question: What are the names and characteristics of the four seasons?

Activity Two: Seasons Sense Poem

Key Question: How can the five senses be used to describe the seasons?

Activity Three: Seasons Haiku

Key Question: Write a haiku about a season.

Setting the Scene

As a class, sort everyday objects that reflect the season with which each might be associated. Discuss signs of each season and explore ways that students can tell the seasons are changing.

Resources

Weather: Poems for All Seasons, Lee Bennett Hopkins

Caps, Hats, Socks, and Mittens: A Book About the Four Seasons, Louise Borden

The Seasons of Arnold's Apple Tree, Gail Gibbons

Focus Web Sites

Earth's Seasons—Zoom Astronomy

http://www.enchantedlearning.com/subjects/astronomy/planets/earth/Seasons.shtml

Google

http://www.google.com

(Keywords: seasons, winter, spring, summer, autumn, solstice, equinox)

Name_____ Date _____

The Reasons for the Seasons

Key Question: What are the names and characteristics of the four seasons?

Directions: Visit the Web sites and answer the questions that follow, using complete sentences.

The Seasons

1. How many seasons are there each year?
   _____

2. What are the names of the seasons?
   _____
   _____

3. About how long does each season last?
   _____

4. Name three changes the seasons bring about.

_____

_____

_____

5. What are equinoxes?

_____

_____

6. What is the winter solstice?

_____

_____

7. What is the summer solstice?

_____

_____

Name_____   Date _____

Seasons Sense Poem

Key Question: How can the five senses be used to describe the seasons?

Directions: Poetry may take many forms. In this activity, a six-line poem will be written, using your five senses. Think about your favorite season and follow the directions for each line below.

Example Seasons Sense Poem:

Summer Is . . .

Summer is teal.
It tastes like black raspberry sherbet.
It smells like coconut oil.
Summer reminds me of sand castles
And sounds like thunderstorms.
Summer feels sticky.

Title: _____ Is . . . (Write your favorite season on the line) _____

Line 1: What color do you think of when you think of your favorite season? _____

Line 2: What is something you can taste in your favorite season? _____

Line 3: What is something you can smell in your favorite season? _____

Line 4: What is something you can see in your favorite season? _____

Line 5: What is something you can hear in your favorite season?_____

Line 6: What is something you can feel in your favorite season, or how does your favorite
        season feel? _____

Now, use these words to write your own poem:

_____ Is . . .

_____ is _____.

It tastes like _____.

It smells like _____.

_____ reminds me of _____.

And sounds like _____.

_____ feels _____.

Name_____   Date _____

Seasons Haiku

Key Question: Write a haiku about a season.

Directions: Haiku is a three-line form of poetry that comes from Japan. These poems focus on nature and follow a special syllable pattern for each of their three lines: five syllables in the first line, seven syllables in the second line, and five syllables in the third line. Think about your favorite season and write your own haiku. Remember—syllables are the parts of a word.

Examples:

Spring

Spring is fun to me

it makes me want to giggle

so hard 'til I cry

Winter Outside

I have a snowflake

that looks like an old big bear

and one big round head

Title: _____

Line 1: _____

Line 2: _____

Line 3: _____

Teacher Note: The haiku examples were written by two of my former students. Special thanks to Lauren (99/00) and Megan T. (00/01).

Weather

Background

The weather can be diverse in different locations around the country. This hunt will allow students to recognize and compare basic weather elements including temperature, wind direction, wind speed, and precipitation.

Objectives

The student will be able to recognize weather patterns from data charts (including temperature, wind direction and speed, and precipitation) and graphs.

The student will be able to explore how different weather conditions may affect plants, animals, food availability, and daily human life.

The Hunt

Activity One: What's the Weather Like Where You Live?

Key Question: How is weather the same or different in two separate locations?

Setting the Scene

As a whole class, create a semantic map detailing information your students associate with the word "weather." Discuss the terms "temperature," "wind speed," and "wind direction" to insure background knowledge is in place to complete this hunt.

Resources

Wild Weather Soup, Caroline Formby

The Magic School Bus Gets Wet All Over: A Book About the Water Cycle, Patricia Relf

The Magic School Bus Kicks Up A Storm: A Book About Weather, Nancy White, Bruce Degen

The Cloud Book, Tomie dePaola

Focus Web Sites

ZipInfo.com

http://zipinfo.com/search/zipcode.htm

Weather.com

http://www.weather.com

Google

http://www.google.com

(Keywords: weather forecast)

Name_____ Date _____

What's the Weather Like Where You Live?

Key Question: How is weather the same or different in two separate locations?

Directions: We will be tracking weather conditions in our town and another location chosen with your teacher's help.

1. Write the name of your town and state. _____

2. Write the name of the town and state you've chosen. _____

ZipInfo.com

3. Type the city and state in which you live. What is the zip code for your town? _____

4. Type the city and state you've chosen. What is the zip code for that town? _____

Weather.com

Using the zip code information you've found, visit Weather.com each day for five days. Using the table below, record the temperature, wind speed, and wind direction for your town and the town you've chosen.

Name of your town:				Name of other town:		
Zip code of your town:				Zip code of other town:		
Date	Temperature	Wind Speed	Wind Direction	Temperature	Wind Speed	Wind Direction

Extension: With your teacher's help, create a graph to show results from one of the weather elements you list in your table. Older students may try graphing with *Microsoft Excel* or another spreadsheet program. Or, older students may wish to graph one weather element for both towns, and create a double bar or line graph.

Sound

Background

Sound is an energy form that moves in waves or ripples. This hunt is designed to allow your students to explore the characteristics of sound and how it moves.

Objectives

The student will be able to recognize that sound has characteristics.

The student will be able to recognize that sound is an energy form.

The Hunt

Activity One: Do You Hear What I Hear?

Key Question: What different types of waves does sound make?

Activity Two: Incredible Orchestra Instruments

Key Question: What attributes of musical instruments are the same and which are different?

Activity Three: Shhhhh! I'm Trying To Read!

Key Question: What type of invention could prevent sound from escaping?

Activity Four: Music, Music, Everywhere

Key Question: What careers are available in the music industry?

Setting the Scene

Students should participate in several discovery activities prior to beginning this hunt. Student activities, included in the companion sites below, help students to explore the concepts of pitch and understand that sound moves in waves or ripples. As a class, use a KWL chart to launch a discussion of what the class already knows (K), what they want to know (W), and what they've learned (L). Use resource materials available in your library and home for background knowledge.

Resources

The Magic School Bus, Inside the Haunted House video

Meet the Orchestra, Ann Hays

Zin! Zin! Zin!: A Violin, Lloyd Moss

Focus Web Sites

Bill Nye: Nye Labs Episode #12

http://www.billnye.com/

(Click on Episode Guides: Physical Science: Physics: Sound)

Energy in the Air: Sounds from the Orchestra

http://library.thinkquest.org/5116/

Name_____ Date _____

Do You Hear What I Hear?

Key Question: What different types of waves does sound make?

Directions: Visit the Web sites listed below and answer the questions that follow.

Bill Nye the Science Guy—Nye Labs Episode Guide #12 "Sound"

1. When you drop a rock into a pond or lake, something happens to the water. Sound moves a lot like the water. What words might describe the way sound moves?

   _____

   _____

2. How are sizes of waves for loud sounds different from sizes of waves for soft sounds?

   _____

   _____

3. Scientists use what special instrument to see the waves that sound makes?

   _____

   _____

Energy in the Air: Sounds from the Orchestra

4. Click the "Sound is Energy" link. What is another name for a musical sound?

   _____

5. Different types of sounds have different types of sound waves. What is different about the sound waves for a soft, high note versus the sound waves for a loud, high note?

   _____

   _____

6. What does the word "pitch" mean? _____

   _____

7. Think about some instruments you know. What are some different ways these instruments make sounds? _____

   _____

8. Write two interesting facts you learned from this site._____

   _____

Name_____ Date _____

Incredible Orchestra Instruments

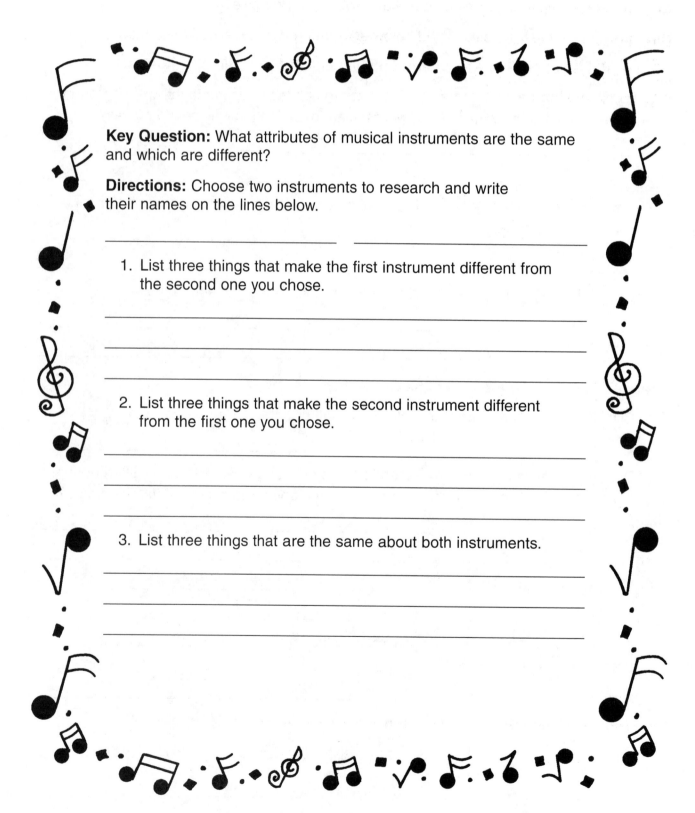

Key Question: What attributes of musical instruments are the same and which are different?

Directions: Choose two instruments to research and write their names on the lines below.

_____   _____

1. List three things that make the first instrument different from the second one you chose.

   _____

   _____

   _____

2. List three things that make the second instrument different from the first one you chose.

   _____

   _____

   _____

3. List three things that are the same about both instruments.

   _____

   _____

   _____

Name_____   Date _____

Shhhhh! I'm Trying to Read!

Key Question: What type of invention could prevent sound from escaping?

Directions: You just learned a new song in school and you want to practice singing it at home. Your brother or sister is trying to read in the next room. In the space below, illustrate an invention that would allow you to keep singing, but keeps the sound from reaching the room where your brother or sister is trying to read. Write a caption that tells about your illustration.

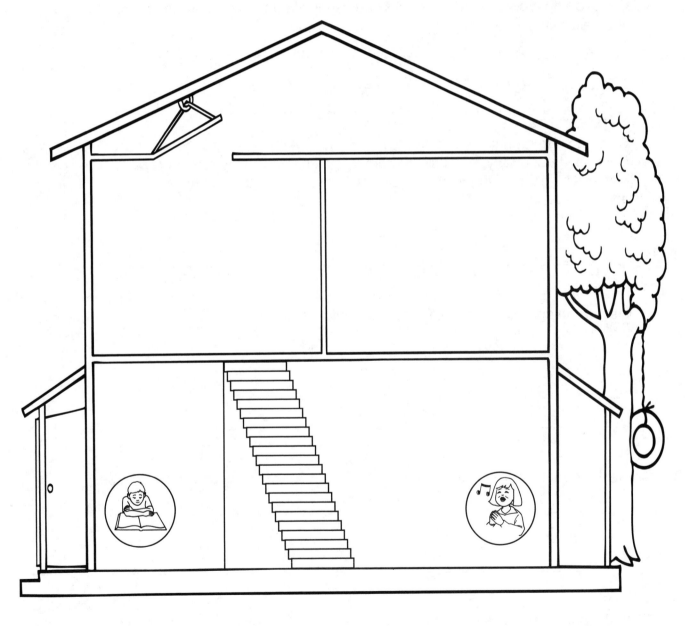

Caption: _____

_____

Name_____ Date _____

Music, Music, Everywhere

Key Question: What careers are available in the music industry?

Directions: There are many types of careers from which adults can choose that have to do with music. This activity will help you find out about three of them. Use an atlas or United States map. Choose one state and write its name and capital on the lines below.

State _____ State Capital _____

1. Choose one type of music business you would like to research. Place a check on the line next to the kind of business to show your choice.

   _____ A music business that fixes instruments

   _____ A music business that sells instruments

   _____ A music business that teaches instrument lessons

2. Using a search engine's Internet yellow pages (yahoo.com is a good choice), select your city and state, and type "music instrument sales," "music instrument repair," or "music instrument lessons" in the search box. Choose one of the businesses listed and write the address below.

   _____

   _____

   _____

3. List four things about yourself that you would like to tell the person to whom you will be writing.

   _____

   _____

   _____

   _____

4. List four questions you would like to ask the owner of the business you chose.

   _____

   _____

   _____

   _____

5. With your teacher's help, write a friendly letter to the business you found on the Internet. Use the list of things about you and questions you wrote to help you write your paragraphs.

Tigers, Tigers, and More Tigers

Background

For many years, the tiger has been a symbol of strength and beauty. Book characters, sports teams, and television commercials have used the tiger in their names and visual presentations. In the natural world, there are fish, insects, and reptiles that are named after the tiger. Using Internet resources, students explore information about the tiger and its namesakes, and then compare and contrast the tiger with a fish, insect, or reptile that has tiger in its name.

Objectives

The student will explore the characteristics and habitats of the wild Asian tiger.

The student will read about other fish, insects, and reptiles named after tigers.

The student will create a Venn diagram illustrating similarities and differences between the tiger and one "tiger" fish, insect, or reptile.

The Hunt

Activity One: Terrific Tigers

> **Key Question:** What are the characteristics and habitats of wild Asian tigers?

Activity Two: Tigers, Tigers, and Tigers, Oh my!

> **Key Question:** What other fish and reptiles are named after the tiger?

Activity Three: Tigers . . . Same or Different?

> **Key Question:** What is the same and what is different about the tiger and one of its namesakes?

Focus Web Sites

5 Tigers

> **http://www.savethetigerfund.org/Directory/kids.htm**

Enchanted Learning: Tiger Shark

> **http://www.enchantedlearning.com/subjects/sharks/species/Tigershark.shtml**

Mexican Tiger Rat Snake

> **http://www.whozoo.org/Anlife2001/jeffcate/JeffCates_MexicanTigerRatSnake.html**

Google

> **http://www.google.com**

(Keywords: tiger, tiger shark, tiger snake)

Name_____ Date _____

Terrific Tigers

Key Question: What are the characteristics and habitats of wild Asian tigers?

Directions: Let's find some important facts about the tiger. Read about the wild tiger. Find information on the Web site to fill in the blanks and answer the questions below.

1. What do tigers like to eat? _____ _____ _____ _____ _____	2. Shade in the places where tigers live. 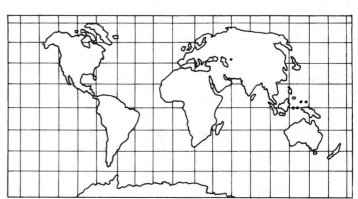
3. Draw a web like this one on another sheet of paper. Fill in information about each of the topics. 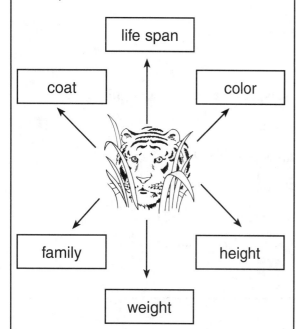	4. Color the place where tigers like to live. 

Name_____ Date _____

Tigers, Tigers, and Tigers, Oh My!

Key Question: What other fish and reptiles are named after the tiger?

Directions: There are other living things that have tiger characteristics. These fish and reptiles have tiger in their names. Explore the companion Web sites and read about the tiger shark, tiger moth, and tiger snakes. Fill in any information that you find in the table below. Draw and color pictures of the shark and snake in the circles below the table.

Name	Color	Size	Diet	Habitat
Shark				
Snakes				

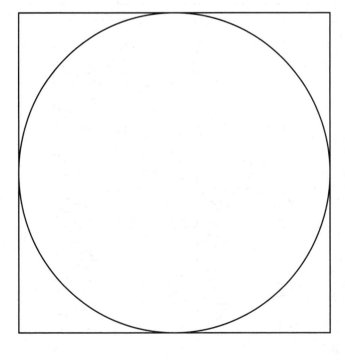 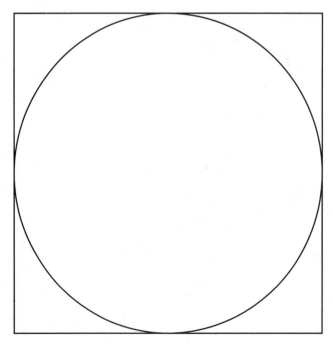

_____   _____

Name_____ Date _____

Tigers...Same or Different?

Key Question: What is the same and what is different about the tiger and one of its namesakes?

Directions: Why do you think that the shark and snake were named after the tiger? See if you can uncover things that are the same and things that are different about the tiger and one of its namesakes. Choose the shark or snake and write its name on the line over the circle. Compare it with the tiger and fill in the Venn diagram using the information you collected in activities one and two. Write the things that are the same in the center of the two circles; put the things that are different outside this middle area under the appropriate heading.

Tiger: _____   Tiger Namesake: _____

Things about   Things about the
the tiger   tiger namesake

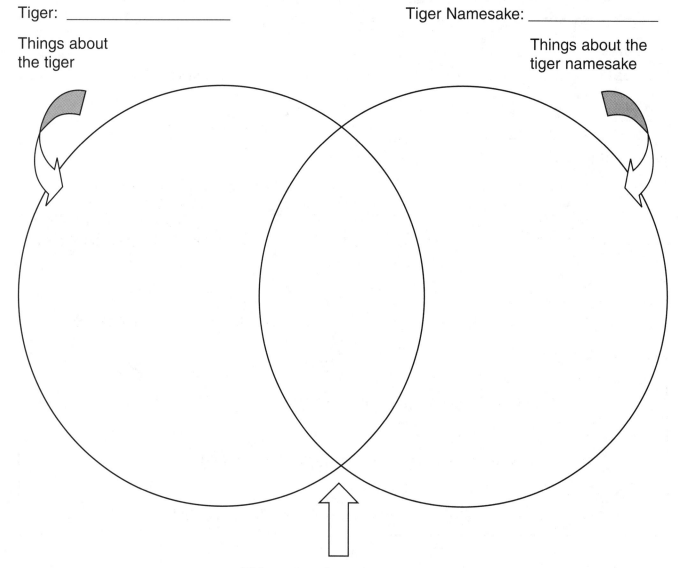

Things they have in common.

Matter

Background

Matter is all around us and takes different forms. This hunt is designed to help your students recognize the three forms of matter, understand that matter changes, and identify basic concepts about the structure of matter.

Objectives

The student will recognize that there are three forms of matter.

The student will identify changes in matter.

The student will be able to describe matter and its particles.

The Hunt

Activity One: All About Matter

Key Question: What are the types and properties of matter?

Activity Two: Matter Similes

Key Question: How can similes be used to compare and describe objects?

Activity Three: Is it Solid or is it Liquid?

Key Question: How can decisions about the properties of matter be made?

Setting the Scene

As a class, make a list of everyday objects. As children offer items for the list, the teacher should separate them into columns, grouping solids, liquids, or gases, but not label the columns. After brainstorming, ask students what they notice about the items in each column and why they were placed together. Challenge them to discover the correct titles for the columns as they investigate the Web sites.

Resources

Bartholomew and the Oobleck, Dr. Seuss

What is the World Made Of?: All About Solids, Liquids, and Gases, Kathleen Weidner Zoehfeld

Focus Web Sites

Chem4Kids.com: Matter

http://www.chem4kids.com/files/matter_intro.html

What Is Matter?

http://www.nyu.edu/pages/mathmol/textbook/whatismatter.html

States of Matter

http://www.harcourtschool.com/activity/states_of_matter/index.html

Google

http://www.google.com

(Keywords: matter, solid, liquid, gas)

Name_____ Date _____

All About Matter

Key Question: What are the types and properties of matter?

Directions: Answer the questions using complete sentences.

Matter

1. What is matter?

   _____

   _____

2. Matter takes different forms. What are three forms you already know about?

   _____

   _____

3. Draw a picture of an example of each of the three forms of matter you know about. Write a caption under each picture to explain it.

_____   _____   _____

_____   _____   _____

_____   _____   _____

All About Matter *(cont.)*

What is Matter?

4. People can describe objects four different ways. How do people describe objects?

_____

_____

5. What does a property describe?

_____

_____

6. All objects have two properties. Name them.

_____

7. All objects are made of very small parts you can't see with your eyes. What are these parts called?

_____

_____

States of Matter

8. Look at each form of matter to see what the particles look like. Draw a picture of the particles in each form of matter. Label each drawing with a caption to explain what form of matter it is.

_____   _____   _____

_____   _____   _____

_____   _____   _____

Name_____ Date _____

Matter Similes

Key Question: How can similes be used to compare and describe objects?

Directions: A simile compares two things, using the word "as" to connect them. For example, when describing a feather, you might write: "A feather feels as soft as cotton." Think about what you know about the items listed below. Use your five senses and think of a simile to describe each item. Fill in the blanks to complete the similes.

1. Maple syrup looks as _____ as _____

   smells as _____ as _____

   tastes as _____ as _____

   feels as _____ as _____

2. Candy-coated chocolates look as _____ as _____

   smell as _____ as _____

   taste as _____ as _____

   feel as _____ as _____

3. Ice cubes look as _____ as _____

   taste as _____ as _____

   feel as _____ as _____

   smell as _____ as _____

4. Choose your own item and write at least three similes, using any of your five senses to describe it.

   _____

   _____

   _____

Name_____ Date _____

Is it Solid or is it Liquid?

Key Question: How can I decide if matter is a solid or a liquid?

Directions: After listening to the story, *Bartholomew and the Oobleck*, you can make your own oobleck, using the recipe below:

1 box cornstarch

1 1/2 cups water

green food coloring

Put the cornstarch in a bowl. Add a few drops of green food coloring. Pour the water in slowly, mixing with your hand. Stop adding water when the mixture becomes lumpy. Squeeze the mixture through your fingers. Think about what you have learned about liquids and solids. Do you think this mixture is a liquid or a solid? Explain why you think the way you do.

Clean-up Note: Cornstarch will clog your sink! Do not wash the mixture down the drain! Let the mixture harden, place it in a baggie, and put it in the trash.

Energy

Background

There are many types of energy. This hunt will allow students to explore renewable and non-renewable forms of energy.

Objectives

The student will be able to recognize that there are different types of energy.

The student will be able to understand basic energy types and sources.

The Hunt

Activity One: Exploring Energy

Key Question: What types of renewable energy are available?

Setting the Scene

As a class, have students write a response in a science journal to "I think energy is . . . ." After completing the hunt, have students write an additional journal entry, explaining what they have learned. Students may also try one of the energy activities listed in the companion sites.

Resources

The Magic School Bus "Gets Energized," Scholastic video

Focus Web Sites

EIA Kids Page

http://www.eia.doe.gov/kids/energyfacts/index.html

Google

http://www.google.com

(Keywords: energy, renewable, nonrenewable)

Name_____ Date _____

Exploring Energy

Key Question: What types of renewable energy are available?

Directions: Answer the questions that follow. Use complete sentences for all your answers.

Nonrenewable Energy

1. What is nonrenewable energy?

2. What are four kinds of nonrenewable energy?

   _____

   _____

3. What is the danger of using nonrenewable energy?

   _____

   _____

   _____

Renewable Energy

4. What is renewable energy?

   _____

   _____

5. What are the main kinds of renewable energy?

   _____

   _____

6. Why is using renewable energy a good idea?

   _____

   _____

Exploring Energy *(cont.)*

Energy from the Sun

7. What is solar energy used for?

_____

_____

_____

Energy from the Wind

8. What are modern windmills called?

_____

9. What do these windmills create?

_____

_____

_____

10. What are wind farms?

_____

_____

Energy from Plants and Animals—Biomass

11. What is the most common kind of biomass?

_____

12. What is ethanol made from?

_____

13. What is biodiesel made from?

_____

_____

Soil

Background

Children love dirt! This hunt will allow children to explore different types of soil, understand how soil is formed, and recognize that weather elements may affect the physical features of a terrain.

Objectives

The student will be able to recognize that soil is made up from weathered rock and decomposed organic material.

The student will be able to recognize that there are different soil types.

The student will understand the relationship between the weather elements and physical features of a terrain.

The Hunt

Activity One: Soil Detective…What's in There Anyway?

Key Question: What forces are involved in creating soil?

Setting the Scene

As a class, look at samples of three different soil types. Decide upon the characteristics that are the same and those that are different. Plant a bean sprout seed in each type of soil. Predict the seed's growth over a two-week period, and compare with the actual growth of the plants in each type of soil. Children may also use the activities listed in the companion sites to explore the role decomposition plays in creating soil.

Resources

There's A Hair In My Dirt!: A Worm's Story, Gary Larson

Focus Web Sites

Is Soil Made Through Magic?

http://www.nrcs.usda.gov/feature/education/squirm/skQ1.html

What Does the Weather Do to Soil?

http://www.nrcs.usda.gov/feature/education/squirm/skQ3.html

What on Earth is Soil?

http://www.epa.gov/gmpo/edresources/soil.html

Name_____ Date _____

Soil Detective...What's in There Anyway?

Key Question: What forces are involved in creating soil?

Directions: Visit the Web sites below and answer the questions that sentences for all your answers.

Is Soil Made Through Magic?

1. Where does soil come from?

_____

What Does the Weather do to Soil?

2. What happens to rocks when the weather becomes hot? What happens to rocks when the weather becomes cold?

_____

_____

3. What happens to rocks over time, as the weather continues to change from hot to cold?

_____

_____

4. What else can cause rocks to break apart?

_____

_____

What on Earth is Soil?

5. Soil makes up which layer of our planet?

_____

_____

6. About how many years can it take to form one inch of topsoil?

_____

_____

7. How many types of soil have scientists identified in the United States?

_____

_____

Fossils

Background
Children are always fascinated with imprints left in rocks that tell of life long ago. This hunt will help children explore fossils and consider the type of environment that created them.

Objectives
The student will recognize that soil is made from weathered rock and decomposed organic material.

The student will identify fossils and the type of environment they lived in (i.e. tropical, aquatic, desert).

The Hunt
    Activity One: Finding Out About Fossils

        Key Question: How are fossils formed?

Setting the Scene:
As a class, complete the "What I Know" and "What I Wonder" section of a KWL chart. After finishing the hunt, the "What I Learned" column may be completed. Children may also create their own fossils, using the activity suggestions found in the companion sites listing.

Resources
Fossils Tell of Long Ago, Aliki

Dinosaur Bones (Let's Read and Find Out), Aliki

Dinosaur Tree, Douglas Henderson

I Dig Fossils: Real Adventure for Kids (1993) video

Focus Web Sites
    Digging into Fossils

        http://imnh.isu.edu/Public/JustForKids/FossilRecord/subm1temp.html

    Fabulous Fossils

        http://www.frsd.k12.nj.us/newman/science/rocks/fabulous.htm

    What is a Fossil?

        http://web.ukonline.co.uk/conker/fossils/what-is-a-fossil.htm

    Google

        http://www.google.com

(Keyword: fossil)

Name_____ Date _____

Finding Out About Fossils

Key Question: How are fossils formed?

Directions: Answer the questions that follow, using complete sentences.

Digging Into Fossils

1. What are fossils?

   _____

   _____

2. What language does the word *fossil* come from? What does the word mean in this language?

   _____

   _____

3. Special kinds of scientists study fossils. What are these special scientists called?

   _____

   _____

Fabulous Fossils

4. When an animal or plant dies, it leaves behind certain parts of itself. What parts of plants and animals are left behind?

   _____

   _____

5. The parts left behind may become covered with mud. How does the mud turn into a fossil?

   _____

   _____

6. Where are two places you can find fossils?

   _____

   _____

Finding Out About Fossils *(cont.)*

What is a Fossil?

7. Fossils are the remains of animals and plants left from long ago. What kinds of animal or plant parts may become fossils?

_____

_____

_____

_____

Fossil Found

Imagine that you found a fossil. You might have found it in your backyard, at the beach, or on a camping trip. Draw a picture of the fossil you found and then write two sentences about where it came from.

_____

_____

Lunar Phases

Background

As the moon moves around the earth each month, its shape changes continuously in our perception. This hunt will allow children to explore how the moon appears at different times of the month during lunar phases.

Objectives

The student will be able to describe the composition and structure of the universe and the earth's place in it.

The student will be able to understand lunar phases.

The Hunt

Activity One: Birthday Moon

Key Question: What are the phases of the moon?

Activity Two: Lunar Phases Birthday Tally

Key Question: How can a graph be used to show the phases of the moon for specific dates?

Activity Three: Lunar Noun Poem

Key Question: Create a poem about the moon.

Setting the Scene

As a class, use a Venn diagram to compare the moon with the sun. Revise the similarities and differences as children discover new information during the hunt.

Resources

Papa, Please Get the Moon for Me, Eric Carle

Full Moon Stories: Thirteen Native American Legends, Eagle Walking Turtle

Focus Web Sites

The Phases of the Moon

http://www.enchantedlearning.com/subjects/astronomy/moon/Phases.shtml

StarDate Online—Moon Phase Calculator

http://stardate.org/nightsky/moon/

Google

http://www.google.com

(Keywords: moon phases, moon phase calculator)

Name_____ Date _____

Birthday Moon

Key Question: What are the phases of the moon?

Directions: Complete the activities below.

The Phases of the Moon

1. The way the moon looks changes during different times of each month. Describe what the moon looks like in each of the four phases below. Draw a picture of what the moon looks like in each phase next to your description.

New Moon:

Full Moon:

First Quarter:

Last Quarter:

The Moon When You Were Born

2. Write the date of your birthday.

   _____

3. Write the month of your birthday with numbers.
   (Example: January =01, March =03)

   _____

4. Write the year you were born.

   _____

5. Find out what the phase of the moon was like on the day and in the year you were born. Use the descriptions you drew and wrote to help you. Then, complete this sentence:
   On the day and in the year I was born, the phase of the moon was

   _____

Name_____   Date _____

Lunar Phases Birthday Tally

Key Question: How can a graph be used to show the phases of the moon for specific dates?

Directions: Ask your classmates what the moon looked like on the day and in the year they were born. Put tally marks in the table below to show the results of your survey.

New Moon	
First Quarter	
Full Moon	
Last Quarter	

1. Color in the bar graph to show how many students were born in each phase of the moon.

	New Moon	First Quarter	Full Moon	Last Quarter
16				
15				
14				
13				
12				
11				
10				
9				
8				
7				
6				
5				
4				
3				
2				
1				
0				

Extension:
With older primary students, you may wish to complete this graph using *Microsoft Excel* or another spreadsheet program.

Name_____ Date _____

Lunar Noun Poem

Key Question: Create a poem about the moon.

Directions: A noun verse is a poem with a special word pattern. Use the pattern below to help you write a poem about the moon.

Line 1: Write the word "moon" (noun).

Line 2: Write two words describing the moon (adjectives). Separate these words with a comma.

Line 3: Write two words ending in "ing" that show the moon's actions (verbs). Separate these words with a comma.

Line 4: Write the word "moon" (noun) again or think of a synonym for the word moon.

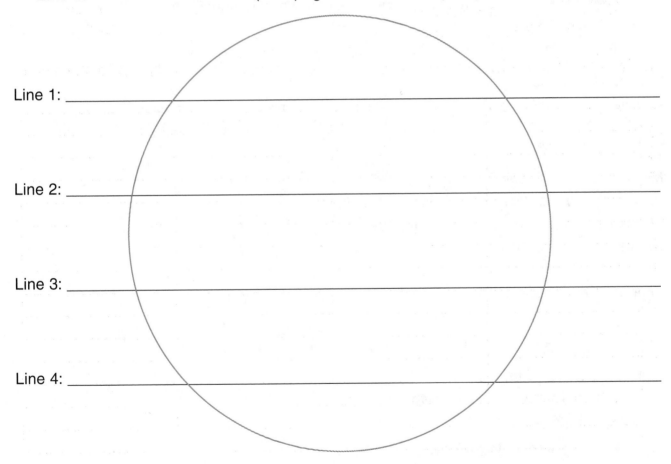

Line 1: _____

Line 2: _____

Line 3: _____

Line 4: _____

Extensions:
Teachers of older primary students may extend this activity to include a quick and easy introduction to a Thesaurus. Remind students that a thesaurus is organized in alphabetical order, just like a dictionary. Choose the verbs from line 3, drop the "ing," and have your students search for synonyms to use in their poems.

It Doesn't Grow on the Grocery Store Shelf

Background

This hunt will allow your students to explore where food comes from and help them to understand the importance of agriculture.

Objectives

The student will understand that communities form near critical natural resources.

The student will be able to identify farming as an important resource.

The student will understand that farming can be the basis of a community's economy.

The Hunt

Activity One: Farms and Dairies

Key Question: What activities happen on farms and why is farming important?

Activity Two: What's Your Favorite Farm Animal?

Key Question: Write an animal story using a published story as a model.

Setting the Scene

As a class, create a KWL chart. Brainstorm what your students know about farming (K column), what they wonder about farming (W column), and what they learned (L column) about farming after completing the hunt.

Resources

Junie B. Jones Has a Peep in Her Pocket, Barbara Parks

Click, Clack, Moo: Cows That Type, Doreen Cronin

The Milk Makers, Gail Gibbons

Milk From Cow To Carton, Aliki

Growing Seasons, Elsie Lee Splear

If You Give a Pig a Pancake, Laura Numeroff

Focus Web Sites

USDA Agriculture for Kids

http://www.fsa.usda.gov/ca/agforkids.htm

USDA Farm Facts

http://www.fsa.usda.gov/ca/kidsfacts.htm

Dairy Facts

http://www.mda.state.mi.us/kids/pictures/dairy/index.html

Google

http://www.google.com

(Keywords: USDA, agriculture, farm facts, dairy facts)

Hunting for Science: Agriculture

Name_____ Date _____

Farms and Dairies

Key Question: What activities happen on farms and why is farming important?

Directions: Answer the questions that follow. Use complete sentences for your answers.

Farm Service Agency for Kids

1. Why are American farmers important?

   _____
   _____
   _____
   _____
   _____

2. About how many farms are in the United States?

   _____

3. What does the Farm Service Agency do?

   _____
   _____
   _____
   _____
   _____

Fun Facts

4. Which state has been the number one agricultural state for more than 50 years?

   _____

5. How many glasses of milk can one cow produce in its lifetime?

   _____

Farms and Dairies *(cont.)*

6. Are pumpkins considered to be fruits or vegetables?

   _____

   _____

7. Read about pigs, artichokes, carrots, or potatoes. Write at least four interesting facts you learned from your reading on this Web site.

   _____

   _____

   _____

   _____

Dairy Facts—From the Farm to You!

8. What do cows eat and drink? _____

   _____

9. What is silage? _____

   _____

10. About how long does it take for a cow to be milked? _____

    _____

11. About how many times a day is a cow milked? _____

    _____

12. Name your favorite farm animal on the line below. Then, draw a picture of that animal in the box. _____

Name_____ Date _____

What's Your Favorite Farm Animal?

Key Question: Write an animal story using a published story as a model.

Directions: After listening to or reading *If You Give a Pig a Pancake*, think about another farm animal you know. Use the planner below to help create your own retelling of this story.

Name a farm animal:_____

What I Will Give My Farm Animal	What Happens Next

Children Around the World

Background

It can be very interesting to find out facts about another country and its culture. This hunt will allow students to consider a variety of aspects of daily life from perspectives of children in other countries.

Objectives

The student will understand that daily life in other countries may be different from our own.

The student will describe the food, school, and recreational activities of children in other countries.

The student will compare aspects of daily life between different locations.

The Hunt

Activity One: Students of the World

Key Question: What is life like for students in another country?

Activity Two: Children: Alike or Different?

Key Question: How is your life the same and how is it different from a student in another country?

Activity Three: Folk Tales Around the World

Key Question: Why are folk tales similar in different cultures?

Activity Four: Around the World Communication!

Key Question: What are some ways to communicate with students in another country?

Setting the Scene

As a class, create a chart to show activities of your daily lives. Include what your school is like, the kinds of foods you like to eat, and how you play. Discuss how this may be different in other countries.

Resources

Clever Katya: A Fairy Tale from Old Russia, Mary Hoffman

Count Your Way Through Brazil, James Haskins

West Africa: Ghana (Ancient and Living Cultures), Myra Herr and Christopher Ronan

Tigers At Twilight, Mary Pope Osborne

Savitri: A Tale of Ancient India, Aaron Shepard

Focus Web Sites

Cool Planet—Wake Up, World!

http://www.oxfam.org.uk/coolplanet/kidsweb/wakeup/

The Names Site

http://www.baby-names-meanings.com/

Google

http://www.google.com

(Keywords: international child "day in the life," name meaning)

Name_____ Date _____

Students of the World

Key Question: What is life like for students in another country?

Directions: Learn about the life of a child from another country. Answer the questions that follow using complete sentences.

1. What is the child's name? _____
   _____

2. Where does he or she live? _____
   _____
   _____

3. What does his or her name mean?_____
   _____
   _____

4. What is school like for this child? _____
   _____
   _____
   _____

5. What kind of food does this child eat? _____
   _____
   _____
   _____

6. How does this child play? _____
   _____
   _____
   _____

The Names Site

7. Try to find the meaning of your first name. Click the rectangle, boy or girl, which would include your first name. These are organized in alphabetical order. Scroll through the list. Write your first name on the line below, and then write what your name means. If your name is not included, write that it was not on the list.

   _____

Name_____ Date _____

Children: Alike or Different?

Key Question: How is your life the same and how is it different from a student in another country?

Directions: Look back at the information you gathered on page 49. Compare your school, what you eat, and how you play with a child from another country. Create a drawing in each box to show different parts of your lives, being careful to look at the heading. Write a sentence to go with each illustration to explain what you have drawn.

Your Name:	Name and Country of Child:
Your School:	Child's School:
Your Food:	Child's Food:
Your Play:	Child's Play:

Name_____ Date _____

Folk Tales Around the World

Key Question: Why are folk tales similar in different cultures?

Directions: Read or listen to the versions of Cinderella listed below. Compare one of the stories with the Cinderella version from our country, using the table below.

Mufaro's Beautiful Daughters: An African Tale, John Steptoe

Baba Yaga and Vasilisa the Brave, Marianna Mayer (A Russian Cinderella)

The Enchanted Anklet: A Cinderella From India, Lila Mehta

The Day It Snowed Tortillas, Joe Hayes (Little Gold Star-Spanish Cinderella)

	Our Cinderella	Other Cinderellas
Character		
Settings		
Problem		
Solution		
Conclusion		

Name_____ Date _____

Around the World Communication!

Key Question: What are some ways to communicate with students in another country?

Directions: Imagine that you are going to write a letter to the child whose life you learned about. Think about what you would tell this child and what you would like to ask him or her. On the planner below, write what you would include in your letter.

1. List at least five things you'd like to tell a child living in another country about yourself.

   _____
   _____
   _____
   _____
   _____

2. List at least five questions you would like to ask a child living in another country.

   _____
   _____
   _____
   _____
   _____

Where in the World is Your Town?

Background

Geography is often an abstract concept for young children. This hunt will allow your students to explore your town and compare it with another town that has the same name and is located in a different part of the United States.

Objectives

The student will understand that a community can be identified by location, people, rules, laws, resources, and history.

The student will learn about the features that are important to a community.

The student will discover that people choose to live in a community for a variety of reasons.

The student will understand that people of many cultures can live together in one community.

The Hunt

Activity One: Your Town

    Key Question: What statistics are available for your town and other cities in the United States?

Activity Two: Share Your Town!

    Key Question: How can a friendly letter be organized?

Setting the Scene

Free Zip Code Look Up **http://www.zipinfo.com/search/zipcode.htm** —Type the name of your city or town in the search box provided. Do not include any information other than the town's name. If your town's name is unique and the search does not return any results, try the search again with the closest bordering town(s). Create a list of all states and zip codes returned from this search.

National Public School Locator **http://nces.ed.gov/ccd/schoolsearch/** —Use this search by simply typing the name of the town and asking for a grade span. Leave all other fields blank. The search will return a listing of all schools and their addresses located in the town you've requested. Copy and paste search results with school listings into a *Microsoft Word* document.

As a class, gather information about your town and state. Make charts showing what types of physical and man-made features are seen in your town, and why people may have moved there. Practice with a map to be certain that students can locate their state and town on a map.

Focus Web Sites

Official City Sites

    http://bigdaddydata.com/usa.php

U.S. Census Bureau—FactFinder Kids Corner

    http://factfinder.census.gov/home/en/kids/funfacts/funfacts.html

Google

    http://www.google.com

(Keywords: city and state names, U.S. Census)

Name_____ Date _____

Your Town

Key Question: What statistics are available for your town and other cities in the United States?

Directions: Answer the questions that follow. Use complete sentences for all your answers.

Official City Sites

1. Go to the United States Web site and choose the state you'd like to search. Then choose the name of the town you would like to search. What is the name of the town?

   _____

2. How many people live in your town? (**Hint:** Look at "Local Population")

   _____

3. What year was the number of people living in your town counted on this Web site?

   _____

4. What is the name of the county your town is located in?

   _____

United States Census Bureau Kids' Corner

5. A census is a counting of the number of people who live in a place. This census was done in the year 2000. How many people were living in your state in the year 2000?

   _____

6. Compare the population from the year 2000 with the population from 1990. How many more people lived in your state in the year 2000 than in the year 1990? Use the space below to show your math work.

   _____

Show your work here.

Your Town *(cont.)*

How Far is it?

7. Search your town and state along with the other town and state you found that shares your town's name (Example: Milford, PA and Milford, TX).

   _____

8. How many miles is it between the two towns?

   _____

9. Go to "Driving Distance and Directions." How long would it take to get from your town to the one that shares its name with yours if you were driving?

   _____

10. According to this Web site, how many people live in your town?

    _____

11. According to this Web site, how many people live in the town that shares its name with yours?

    _____

12. Compare the town's populations. How many more people live in one town than the other? Show your math work in the space provided.

```
Show your work here.



```

States and Capitals

13. Click on your state. What year did your state become a member of the United States?

14. What is the name of your state capital?

    _____

15. What kind of farm products does your state produce?

    _____

16. What is your state's nickname? Why is that nickname used? _____

    _____

17. How did your state get its name?

    _____

    _____

Name_____   Date _____

Share Your Town!

Key Question: How can a friendly letter be organized?

Directions: With your teacher's help, choose a school located in a town that shares its name with yours, or a town located nearby, in a different location of the United States. Use the planner below to organize some ideas to help you write a friendly letter to a class that is the same grade as yours in the school. After completing the planner, follow your teacher's directions for writing the friendly letter.

1. List at least four things you would like to tell about yourself:

   _____

   _____

   _____

   _____

2. Explain why you are writing to this class in a town that shares its name with yours, or one that is located nearby.

   _____

   _____

   _____

   _____

3. List at least three interesting facts about your town. Use information you gathered from the hunt activity, or things about your town you may already know.

   _____

   _____

   _____

   _____

4. List at least four interesting facts about your state. Use information you gathered from the hunt activity or things about your state you may already know.

   _____

   _____

   _____

   _____

Family Connections

Background

Comparing an older adult family member's life experiences to your primary student's interests and activities can be very interesting. This hunt will allow your student to construct a simple family tree, conduct an interview, and compare aspects of daily life.

Objectives

The student will understand that all families have a history.

The student will recognize that aspects of daily life may change over time.

The Hunt

Activity One: Family Tree

Key Question: How can information about a family be organized?

Activity Two: Where in the World?

Key Question: What is the most common birthplace of the class' family members?

Activity Three: Transportation Tally

Key Question: What was the most common mode of transportation to school in the past?

Activity Four: Your Life, My Life

Key Question: How are life experiences the same and how are they different for older and younger family members?

Setting the Scene

As a class, discuss favorite games, methods of traveling to school, where children were born, etc. Ask the students if they think these things may have been different for their grandparents or older relatives. Follow up with discussion about the class' interview results.

Resources

My First Family Tree, Catherine Bruzzone

Tigger's Family Tree (Winnie the Pooh First Readers, 20), Isabel Gaines

The Family Tree Detective: Cracking the Case of Your Family's Story, Ann Douglas

Focus Site

Family Tree

http://projects.edtech.sandi.net/kimbrough/pilgrimlife/familytree.html

Google

http://www.google.com

(Keywords: family tree template)

Name_____   Date _____

Family Tree

Key Question: How can information about a family be organized?

Directions: Visit the Family Tree Web site. Print a copy of the family tree that appears. Ask your family to help you fill in the correct information. Choose one of the oldest adults in your family and ask them the questions below.

Write the name of the adult you spoke to and how they are related to you.

_____

1. Where were you born? _____

2. What was school like when you were my age?

   _____
   _____
   _____
   _____

3. What did you do for fun when you were my age?

   _____
   _____
   _____
   _____

4. Did you have a favorite game? What was it called and how did you play it?

   _____
   _____
   _____

5. How did you travel to school when you were my age?

   _____

6. Write one question of your own you would like to ask the person you are interviewing and then write that person's answer.

   _____
   _____
   _____

Name _____ Date _____

Where in the World?

Key Question: What is the most common birthplace of the class' family members?

Directions: Look at the interview you completed with an older adult family member. As a class, review the locations of the seven continents and tally where the family members were born. Complete the graph to show the tally results.

Where We Were Born

North America	
South America	
Europe	
Asia	
Africa	
Australia	
Antarctica	

	North America	South America	Europe	Asia	Africa	Australia	Antarctica
17							
16							
15							
14							
13							
12							
11							
10							
9							
8							
7							
6							
5							
4							
3							
2							
1							

Extension: Older students may wish to create a graph using *Microsoft Excel* or another spreadsheet program. Or, a double bar graph may be created comparing the student with the person interviewed.

Name_____ Date _____

Transportation Tally

Key Question: What was the most common mode of transportation to school in the past?

Directions: Look at the interview you completed with an older adult family member. As a class, tally how those people traveled to school. Complete the bar graph to show the tally results.

How We Traveled To School

Bus	
Car	
Walk	
Bicycle	
Train	
Other	

	Bus	Car	Walk	Bicycle	Train	Other
19						
18						
17						
16						
15						
14						
13						
12						
11						
10						
9						
8						
7						
6						
5						
4						
3						
2						
1						
	Bus	Car	Walk	Bicycle	Train	Other

Extension: Older students may wish to create a graph using *Microsoft Excel* or another spreadsheet program. Or, a double bar graph may be created comparing the student with the person interviewed.

Name_____ Date _____

Your Life, My Life

Key Question: How are life experiences the same and how are they different for older and younger family members?

Directions: Look at the interview you completed with an older adult family member. In the boxes below, draw pictures to compare parts of your life with your family member.

You	Adult Family Member You Interviewed
Favorite Game	Favorite Game
Traveling to School	Traveling to School
Something I Do for Fun	Something he/she Does for Fun

Shapes and Symmetry

Background

Shapes always fascinate children. Recognizing basic shapes is an important skill for primary students. This hunt will allow your students to explore two and three-dimensional shapes and identify those figures in real life objects.

Objectives

The student will be able to name geometric shapes in two and three dimensions and recognize those figures in real life examples.

The student will be able to identify lines of symmetry in geometric figures and in nature.

The student will understand that shapes can be changed by combining or dividing them.

The Hunt

Activity One: Geometric Shapes

    Key Question: What can be discovered about geometric shapes?

Activity Two: Legend of the Tangram

    Key Question: Read and illustrate a story about the tangram.

Activity Three: Make Your Own Tangram

    Key Question: How can tangram shapes be arranged to make a picture?

Resources

Shapes, Shapes, Shapes, Tana Hoban

Sea Shapes, Susie MacDonald

The Wing on a Flea: A Book About Shapes, Ed Emberley

Three Pigs, One Wolf, and Seven Magic Shapes, Grace MacCarone

The Greedy Triangle, Marilyn Burns

Grandfather Tang's Story, Ann Tompert

Focus Web Sites

I C Shapes

    http://www.sci.mus.mn.us/sln/tf/i/icshapes/icshapes.html

Symmetry

    http://library.thinkquest.org/J002441F/symmetry.htm

Geometry Forum Tangram Template

    http://mathforum.org/pom/big.tangram.html

Google

    http://www.google.com

(Keywords: shapes, circle, square, triangle, symmetry, tangram, tangram template)

Name_____ Date _____

Geometric Shapes

Key Question: What can be discovered about geometric shapes?

Directions: Use the Web sites to help you answer the questions that follow.

1. What are three things found around us that have a circle shape?

_____

_____

In the box below, draw three different things that have a circle shape.

2. What are three things found around us that have a square shape?

_____

_____

In the box below, draw three different things that have a square shape.

3. What are three things found around us that have a triangle shape?

_____

_____

In the box below, draw three different things that have a triangle shape.

4. What does it mean if a figure is symmetric?

_____

_____

In the box below, draw three things you see around you that have symmetry.

Name_____ Date _____

Legend of the Tangram

Key Question: Read and illustrate a story about the tangram.

Directions: Read the "Legend of the Tangram" below. Draw what happens in the story in the boxes. Write a caption inside each box to tell about your drawing. Write a number inside each box to show what order the events happened.

Legend of the Tangram

A long time ago in China, there lived a man called Tan. Tan's greatest possession was a fine ceramic tile. One day Tan was carrying his tile to show the emperor. He tripped and the tile fell and broke into seven geometric shapes: two large triangles, a medium size triangle, a square, and a parallelogram. Tan spent the rest of his life trying to put the tile back together again. He was not successful, but he did succeed in creating many different geometric designs. Tan enjoyed creating the designs. His friends also enjoyed trying to re-create his designs. Tan's puzzles, later called tangrams, were passed on through generations and from country to country.

Name_____ Date _____

Make Your Own Tangram

Key Question: How can tangram shapes be arranged to make a picture?

Directions: Create a picture in the space below, using tangram shapes.

Place Values

Background

As students begin working with three-digit numbers, it is important for them to understand the relationships among counting, grouping, and place values. To work effectively with whole numbers, students must comprehend that each place value holds a special significance for the number in that position, for example, the number 7 in the tens place represents 7 tens, or 70. This hunt provides an opportunity for students to identify place values (100, 10, 1), manipulate numbers within this framework, and demonstrate comprehension through games and written exercises.

Objectives

The student will use Internet resources to learn about place values.

The student will explore Web sites that contain exercises and games using place values.

The student will apply new knowledge and strategies to different place values activities.

The student will demonstrate knowledge of place values in written examples.

The Hunt

Activity One: Numbers: Homes Needed!

Key Question: What place values can numbers have?

Activity Two: Number Mix-Up

Key Question: How does a number change when its place or position changes?

Focus Web Sites

AAA Math

http://www.aaamath.com/grade2.html

Place Value Puzzler

http://www.funbrain.com/tens/

Google

http://www.google.com

(Keywords: place value, place value puzzle, place value game)

Name_____   Date _____

Numbers: Homes Needed!

http://www.teachercreated.com/books/3812   Click on page 67, site 1

Key Question: What place values can numbers have?

Directions: Find a home for the numbers below. Draw a line from each number in the center to a group of boxes. Enter the amount that the number stands for in the 100, 10, and 1 place for each number, for example, 7 in the 10s place equals 70. Remember to enter a zero in the box if there are no 100s, 10s, or 1s in the number.

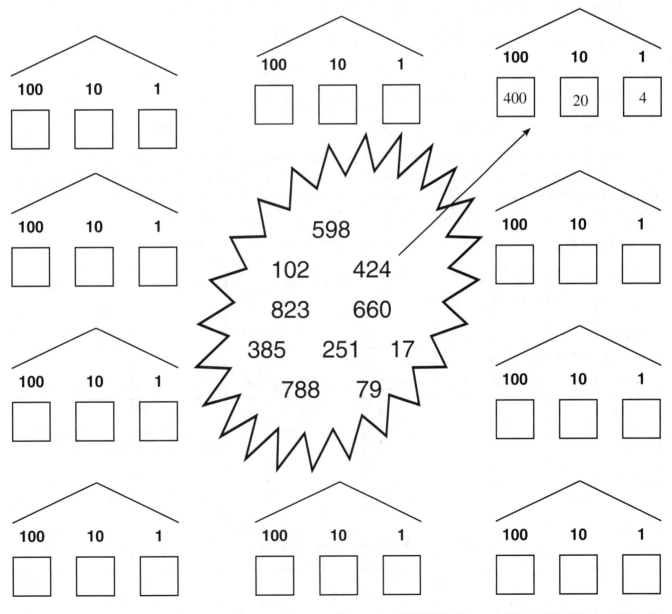

Name_____ Date _____

Number Mix-Up

http://www.teachercreated.com/books/3812   Click on page 68, site 1

Key Question: How does a number change when its place or position changes?

Directions: Find a partner and play a place value game several times. After you finish the game, answer the following questions:

1. How did you know which numbers to click on?

   _____

   _____

   _____

2. What did you learn about the game after you played it more than once?

   _____

   _____

   _____

Think about what you learned from the Web game. Now play your own place values number game! Get a number cube from your teacher and sit with a partner. Take turns rolling one cube and writing the numbers in the blank spaces below. When you complete the game, work with your partner to fill in the hundreds, tens, and ones for your numbers.

Example	2	6	5	265	**two** hundreds	**six** tens	**five** ones
Roll 2:	_____	_____	_____	_____	_____ hundreds	_____ tens	_____ ones
Roll 3:	_____	_____	_____	_____	_____ hundreds	_____ tens	_____ ones
Roll 4:	_____	_____	_____	_____	_____ hundreds	_____ tens	_____ ones
Roll 5:	_____	_____	_____	_____	_____ hundreds	_____ tens	_____ ones
Roll 6:	_____	_____	_____	_____	_____ hundreds	_____ tens	_____ ones

Money

Background

All children learn quickly about the value of money, especially when they find something they want to buy! Being able to identify the different types of coins and paper money is a very basic but essential skill that students must master. This hunt allows students to explore the appearance and value of coins and paper money. Students select items they would like to buy and count the correct amount of money for the purchase. In the final activity, they create their own money with the help of the U.S. Mint.

Objectives

The student will identify coins and paper money.

The student will match coin and dollar combinations to written numbers.

The student will understand the design components of a coin.

The Hunt

Activity One: The Faces of Money

Key Question: What numbers and pictures help identify the value of money?

Activity Two: What Would I Like to Buy?

Key Question: How can money be added together to buy an item?

Activity Three: Create a Coin

Key Question: What important pictures and words appear on a coin?

Teacher's Note: This lesson requires the FLASH plug-in.

Focus Web Sites

The Adventures of Penny

http://www.kidsbank.com/the_story/penny/index.asp

The U.S. Mint—H.I.P. Pocket Change

http://www.usmint.gov/kids/

Primary Games—Spending Spree

http://www.primarygames.com/Spending%20Spree/question_1.htm

Google

http://www.google.com

(Keywords: U.S. Mint, money, kids shopping games, kids primary games)

Name_____ Date _____

The Faces of Money

Key Question: What numbers and pictures help identify the value of money?

Directions: After visiting the Web sites, look at the examples of coins and paper money below. Draw a line from the picture of the money to the number that matches it.

$.05

$5.00

$.01

$.10

$.25

$1.00

Name_____ Date _____

What Would I Like to Buy?

Key Question: How can money be added together to buy an item?

Directions: Go to the Primary Games Web site. Click on the green start arrow and shop for items that you would like to buy. Try to select the correct money needed to buy the item. If you click on the wrong amount, the computer will show you the correct money needed. As you choose each item, write the name of the item and the amount it costs in the table below. After you are finished, draw pictures of the things you bought in the boxes.

Item	Cost

Name_____ Date _____

Create a Coin

Key Question: What important pictures and words appear on a coin?

Directions: Now that you have learned about money, you get to make your own coin! Go to the U.S. Mint Web site and click on the Making Change activity. Follow the directions and create your own coin. When your coin is finished, your teacher may allow you to print one copy of your coin. Color your coin and paste it in the space below. If you are not able to print your coin, draw a picture of it in the space below.

Yippee! Shopping Spree

Background

Children can be savvy little shoppers! This hunt will allow children to select items to purchase, add and total costs of items, and order money amounts.

Objectives

The student will be able to solve addition problems with regrouping in vertical form.

The student will understand information displayed in a table or chart.

The student will be able to display data using a chart or table.

The student will compare money amounts and understand the terms "least" and "most."

The Hunt

Activity One: Shopping Spree

Key Question: How many items can be purchased with a specific amount of money?

Activity Two: Write a Money Story

Key Question: How can a money story be planned?

Setting the Scene:

As a class, review and discuss appropriate use of a decimal and dollar sign. Discuss the terms "least" and "most."

Resources

Arthur's Funny Money, Lillian Hoban

Pigs Will Be Pigs: Fun With Math and Money, Amy Axelrod

Alexander, Who Used to be Rich Last Sunday, Judith Viorst

Focus Web Sites

Great Books for Boys

http://www.randomhouse.com/rhpg/promos/greatbooks/boys/booklist.html

Great Books for Girls

http://www.randomhouse.com/rhpg/promos/greatbooks/girls/booklist.html

Amazon

http://www.amazon.com

Google

http://www.google.com

(Keywords: kids book lists, summer reading list)

Name_____ Date _____

Shopping Spree

Key Question: How many items can be purchased with a specific amount of money?

Congratulations! You have won a shopping spree! Visit Web sites to choose your favorite books, toys, and games. Read all the directions carefully.

Book List _____

1. _____ Go to a Web site with lists of recommended books. Scroll the list and choose five different books you'd like to read. Fill in the title and author for each book.

Book Title	Author's Last Name	Cost of Book

2. Go to Amazon.com. Search the title of each book you chose. Write how much each book costs in the last column of the table above.

3. Search in "Toys & Games." Look in your age group. Click a category of your choice. Choose five different toys or games you'd like to have. Fill in the table below with the information you find about each toy or game.

Name of Game or Toy	Cost of Game or Toy

4. Add the prices of all the items you chose on a separate piece of paper. Be careful to use decimal points and dollar signs. Figure out how much money you spent for all the books, toys, and games.

5. Put the items you chose in order, from least expensive to most expensive.

Name_____ Date _____

Write a Money Story

Key Question: How can a money story be planned?

Directions: After listening to Judith Viorst's *Alexander, Who Used to be Rich Last Sunday*, plan your own Alexander story, using the form below.

1. How much money will you have in the beginning of your story?

    _____

2. Alexander receives his money from his grandparents. In your story, you may receive your money from one or more people. Your money may come from more than one place, as long as it equals the amount you started with. Who or where will your money come from in your story? _____

3. Alexander complains that all he has are bus tokens. What will you have at the beginning and ending of your story? _____

4. Judith Viorst repeats a number of different sentences all through her story. You should include several of these in your own story. List the sentences you would like repeated in your Alexander story. _____

    _____

5. Alexander spends his money in a number of ways. Using the table below, list how you will spend the money in your story. Add your purchases and see if they equal the amount you started with in your story.

Item	Cost
	Total

6. When all of Alexander's money is gone, he tries other ways to get more money. List ways you might try to get more money in your story.

    _____

    _____

7. At the end of the story, Alexander talks about all the things he's left with except for money. List all the things you will be left with at the end of your Alexander story.

    _____

    _____

8. With your teacher's help, and using this story planner to guide you, write your own version of the Alexander story. Your title might be: *(your name), Who Used to be Rich Last Sunday.*

Telling Time

Background

The ability to tell time is an important skill for primary students to master. This hunt allows students to explore the concept of telling time, including a bit of time-measuring history. Students will also explore the concept of telling time as a unit of measurement.

Objectives

The student will understand that telling time has measurable characteristics.

The student will be able to distinguish between digital and analog time.

The Hunt

Activity One: Time

Key Question: What is the history of clocks and why do people have them?

Activity Two: Create a Clock!

Key Question: What shapes, patterns, and figures can be used on a clock?

Setting the Scene

As a class, review parts of an analog clock. Discuss the idea of the passage of time. Make a chart that shows how telling time is used in our daily lives.

Resources

Time (Math Counts), Henry Pluckrose

Clocks and More Clocks, Pat Hutchins

Focus Web Sites

Time

http://www.units.muohio.edu/dragonfly/time/

The History of Clocks

http://www.arcytech.org/java/clock/clock_history.html

Google

http://www.google.com

(Keywords: tell time, accurate time, timekeeping history, clock history)

Name_____ Date _____

Time

Key Question: What is the history of clocks and why do people have them?

Directions: Visit the Web sites listed below and answer the questions that follow each one. Use complete sentences for your answers.

Clocks

1. How did people use the sun to tell time? _____

_____

_____

2. Why don't sundials work at night? _____

_____

_____

_____

3. Why did water clocks work better than sundials? _____

_____

_____

_____

What do you use a clock for? If you didn't have a clock, how would you know when to wake up in the morning? How would you know when it is time for lunch? How would you know when school was over for the day? Write about what your life would be without clocks.

_____

_____

_____

_____

_____

_____

_____

_____

Name_____ Date _____

Create a Clock!

Key Question: What shapes, patterns, and figures can be used on a clock?

Directions: One of the ways people use clocks is for decoration in their homes. Think of how your bedroom might be decorated, or a theme you like. Maybe you like balloons, a certain animal, a certain toy, or a special kind of food. Design your own clock below, using the theme you've chosen. Remember to use your theme for the clock face, and clock hands. Write the time you've drawn on the clock below your drawing.

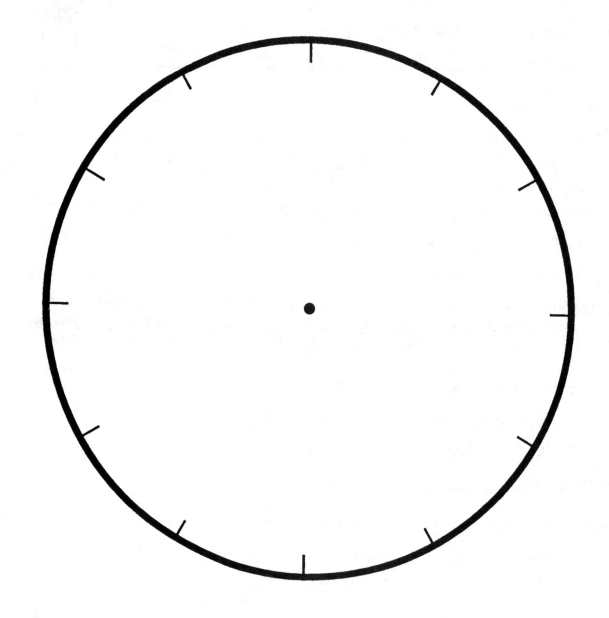

Consonant Clusters

Background

Primary students who are beginning readers and spellers need practice recognizing common clusters and patterns of consonants to develop strong reading and spelling skills. Working with various combinations of consonants assists students in reading, spelling familiar words, and providing tools to decode unfamiliar vocabulary. This Web hunt offers practice for student recognition of initial and ending consonant clusters. Additional activities give students an opportunity to use blended words in their own tales with illustrations from Web sources.

Objectives

The student will use Internet resources to combine common consonant blends and make words.

The student will apply decoding strategies to new words.

The student will explore Web sites that contain rhymes and stories.

The student will write his/her own short tale using blended words.

The Hunt

Activity One: Blend Those Consonants!

Key Question: Which beginning and ending consonants join together to make words?

Activity Two: Tell a Tale

Key Question: Create a short tale with words and pictures from the Internet.

Teacher's Note: This lesson requires the FLASH plug-in.

Focus Web Site

BBC Online—Word Blender

http://www.bbc.co.uk/schools/wordsandpictures/clusters/blender/index.shtml

Internet Public Library Story Hour

http://www.ipl.org/div/kidspace/storyhour/

Ivy's Links to Coloring Pages

http://ivyjoy.com/coloring/coloringlinks.html

Google

http://www.google.com

(Keywords: word blending game, children's stories online, coloring pages)

Hunting for Language Arts: Consonant Clusters

Name_____   Date _____

Blend Those Consonants!

Key Question: Which beginning and ending consonants join together to make words?

Directions: Practice blending words online. Then look at the pictures below. Write the word in the empty box under the picture. Say the word aloud to help you choose the right sounds.

Beginning	Ending
s	ack
ch	ell
sh	alk

Beginning	Ending
cl	ip
sh	ick
bl	ock

Beginning	Ending
br	ock
k	urch
ch	ell

Beginning	Ending
s	ill
bl	ock
br	ing

Beginning	Ending
th	ock
d	irp
cl	oll

Beginning	Ending
br	ack
cr	ick
dr	aw

Name_____   Date _____

Tell a Tale

Key Question: Create a short tale with words and pictures from the Internet.

Directions: Read some online stories. Then, think of a story of your own that you would like to write. Think of a character and an idea for your story. Write your story in the space below. After you have finished writing your story, your teacher will help you search for a coloring sheet that matches your story. Print the sheet and color the picture. Use the picture when sharing your story with the class.

Teacher's Note: Enter a keyword from the story in the search box to find an appropriate coloring sheet.

Example: *Character: Gigi*   *Idea: Soccer*

Gigi aimed the ball at the wall.

She broke the bricks with her kick!

Character for tale: _____

Idea for tale: _____

Tale: _____

_____

_____

_____

_____

_____

_____

Fun With Poetry

Background

Make sure your students don't groan when they hear the word poetry! This hunt will allow your students to understand that poetry does not have to rhyme, can break the conventions of grammar, and can express feelings.

Objectives

The student will be able to identify poetry as a literary device.

The student will identify structures in poetry.

The student will write his or her own poem.

The Hunt

Activity One: Spell a Poem!

Key Question: What is an acrostic poem?

Activity Two: Write Your Own Poem

Key Question: How can one word be used to create a poem?

Setting the Scene

Listen to a variety of poetry, including the poems found in the Resources section. As a class, discuss the poems and make a chart showing things that are the same and different about poems and stories.

Resources

Note: There are literally hundreds of poetry books available. Children amazingly understand the subtleties of humorous poetry, even at a very young age.

Lunch Money and Other Poems About School, Carol Diggory Shields

Did You See What I Saw?: Poems About School, Kay Winters

Somebody Catch My Homework, David L. Harrison

Primarily Poetry—Poetry Lessons For Grades K–3, Lani Steele

Focus Web Sites

Acrostic Poems

http://www.readwritethink.org/materials/acrostic/

Fall Poetry Project

http://myschoolonline.com/folder/0,1872,34898-119831-38-35031,00.html

Google

http://www.google.com

(Keywords: acrostic, acrostic poetry examples)

Name_____ Date _____

Spell a Poem!

Key Question: What is an acrostic poem?

Directions: Answer the questions that follow. Use complete sentences for your answers.

Acrostic

1. What language does the word "acrostic" come from?

   _____

2. In your own words, explain what an acrostic poem is.

   _____

   _____

Acrostic Poetry

3. Read several samples of acrostic poetry written by students your age. Tell what you enjoyed the most about the poems you read.

   _____

   _____

4. Read several more samples of acrostic poetry written by children your age. Copy your favorite acrostic poem to share with your class. Remember to write down the school, town, and state of the poem you chose.

   Name of school: _____

   City or town: _____

   State: _____

   The poem I liked the best: _____

   _____

   _____

   _____

   _____

Name_____ Date _____

Write Your Own Poem

Key Question: How can one word be used to create a poem?

Directions: As a class, in small groups, or on your own, write the name of your favorite season:

1. In five minutes, as a class, in small groups, or on your own, write all the words this season reminds you of. Place these words in a list.

_____

_____

_____

_____

_____

_____

2. Circle your favorite word from the list you created.

3. Write the word you chose in the boxes. Use one letter of the word in each box. Make each letter a capital letter.

4. Write a few words or a sentence on each line. Begin the first word with the letter you wrote on the left edge. Use the season you chose as your theme to help you.

☐ _____

☐ _____

☐ _____

☐ _____

☐ _____

☐ _____

Extension: As a challenge, try using alliteration in your acrostic poem. Each line should have most words begin with the letter found on the left edge of that line.

Meet Paula Danziger

Background

Paula Danziger is the author of the popular *Amber Brown* series. This hunt will allow your students to find out about her background and read helpful tips about becoming a writer.

Objectives

The student will become familiar with the life of a writer.

The student will understand what motivates a writer.

The student will be exposed to writing as a career.

The Hunt

Activity One: Meet Paula Danziger

Key Question: What important information can be discovered about Paula Danziger?

Setting the Scene

As a class, read or listen to selections of Paula Danziger's work listed in the Resources section. The focus Web site also has a link to all of Danziger's work.

Resources

Amber Brown series

Focus Web Site

Meet Paula Danzinger

http://www.scholastic.com/titles/paula/

Book Page Interview: Paula Danzinger

http://www.bookpage.com/9602bp/childrens/pauladanziger.html

Google

http://www.google.com

(Keywords: Paula Danzinger)

Name_____ Date _____

Meet Paula Danziger

Key Question: What important information can be discovered about Paula Danziger?

Directions: Answer the questions that follow. Use complete sentences for all your answers.

Meet Paula Danziger

1. When did Paula Danziger first know she wanted to be a writer?

   _____

   _____

2. Paula Danziger explains that her ideas come from three things. What are they?

   _____

   _____

   _____

3. What are three of the tips Paula Danziger gives to anyone who would like to become a writer?

   _____

   _____

   _____

4. One of Paula Danziger's hobbies is collecting things. What does she like to collect?

   _____

5. Find and read about Paula Danziger's favorite expressions. Write the one you like the best. Tell why you like it.

   _____

   _____

6. What is Paula Danziger's favorite color?

   _____

7. What are two things Paula Danziger feels proud about?

   _____

   _____

Meet Laura Numeroff

Background:

Children enjoy finding out about their favorite authors. This hunt will allow your students to learn about Laura Numeroff, author of *If You Give a Mouse a Cookie*, and other titles.

Objectives

The student will become familiar with the life of a writer.

The student will understand what motivates a writer.

The student will be exposed to writing as a career.

The Hunt

Activity One: Meet Laura Numeroff

Key Question: What important information can be discovered about Laura Numeroff?

Setting the Scene

Laura Numeroff is a favorite author of many young children. Read selections of her work (found in the resources section) before beginning the hunt.

Resources

If You Give a Mouse a Cookie

If You Give a Moose a Muffin

If You Take a Mouse to the Movies

If You Give a Pig a Pancake

What Mommies Do Best, What Daddies Do Best

What Grandmas Do Best, What Grandpas Do Best

The Chicken Sisters

If You Take a Mouse to School

Focus Site

Laura Numeroff's Very Own Web Site

http://www.lauranumeroff.com/

Kids Reads.com: Laura Numeroff

http://www.kidsreads.com/authors/au-numeroff-laura.asp

Google

http://www.google.com

(Keywords: Laura Numeroff)

Name_____ Date _____

Meet Laura Numeroff

Key Question: What important information can be discovered about Laura Numeroff?

Directions: Answer the questions that follow. Use complete sentences for all your answers.

1. Laura Numeroff loves to travel. There are four states she has not visited yet. Which states are they?

   _____

   _____

   _____

2. What kinds of things does Laura Numeroff like to collect?

   _____

   _____

3. What kind of books are Laura Numeroff's favorites? When does she like to read them?

   _____

   _____

4. What are Laura Numeroff's favorite foods?

   _____

5. What three suggestions does Laura Numeroff give to find ideas for writing your own stories?

   _____

   _____

   _____

6. What is the most important thing Laura Numeroff tells children to do when they write a story?

   _____

   _____

   _____

Meet Elvira Woodruff

Background

Elvira Woodruff is an author many children enjoy. This hunt will allow your students to learn more about her as well as receive advice about becoming writers.

Objectives

The student will become familiar with the life of a writer.

The student will understand what motivates a writer.

The student will be exposed to writing as a career.

The Hunt

Activity One: Meet Elvira Woodruff

Key Question: What important information can be discovered about Elvira Woodruff?

Setting the Scene

As a class, read or listen to selections of Elvira Woodruff's work listed in the Resources section. Woodruff was a visitor to our school; her Web site explains how to schedule an author visit. She is a dynamic, enthusiastic speaker and we enjoyed her presentation very much!

Resources

George Washington's Socks

The Memory Coat

A Dragon in My Backpack

Can You Guess Where We're Going?

The Wing Shop

Awfully Short for Fourth Grade

Tubtime

Focus Web Site

Elvira Woodruff's Web Site
http://www.ewoodruff.com/

Elvira Woodruff Biography
http://www.ewoodruff.com/

Google
http://www.google.com
(Keywords: Elvira Woodruff)

Name_____ Date _____

Meet Elvira Woodruff

Key Question: What important information can be discovered about Elvira Woodruff?

Directions: Answer the questions that follow. Use complete sentences for all your answers.

1. How many years has Elvira Woodruff been writing books?

   _____

2. Where was Elvira Woodruff born? What state does she live in now?

   _____

   _____

   _____

3. When Elvira Woodruff is not busy working on her books, there are three other things she likes to do. What are they?

   _____

   _____

   _____

4. Elvira Woodruff lists 10 tips for becoming a writer. List three tips that you like and why you like them.

   _____

   _____

   _____

   _____

   _____

Meet Jane Yolen

Background

Jane Yolen is an author of many children's books. This hunt will allow your students to explore her background and read advice she gives to young writers.

Objectives

The student will become familiar with the life of a writer.

The student will understand what motivates a writer.

The student will be exposed to writing as a career.

The Hunt

Activity One: Meet Jane Yolen

Key Question: What important information can be discovered about Jane Yolen?

Setting the Scene

As a class, read or listen to selections of Jane Yolen's work listed in the Resources section. This lesson can be extended by visiting Web site 3 listed below in the companion sites section. There are links to curriculum guides, additional biographical information, and discussion group participation for classrooms.

Resources

The Emperor and the Kite

Commander Toad and the Space Pirate

Piggins, Picnic With Piggins, Piggins and the Royal Wedding

Owl Moon

Sleeping Ugly

Teacher Note: For a complete list, go to Jane Yolen's Web site, click "For Teachers" and go to "Books By Theme and Age."

Focus Web Site

Focus Web Sites

Jane Yolen's Official Website
http://www.janeyolen.com/

Jane Yolen's FAQs for Kids
http://www.janeyolen.com/faqs.html

Google
http://www.google.com
(Keywords: Jane Yolen)

Name_____ Date _____

Meet Jane Yolen

Key Question: What important information can be discovered about Jane Yolen?

Directions: Answer the questions that follow. Use complete sentences for all your answers.

1. When was Jane Yolen born?

   _____

2. When was Jane Yolen's first success as a writer? What was her story about?

   _____

   _____

   _____

3. What did Jane Yolen's parents do for a living?

   _____

   _____

4. Where does Jane Yolen get ideas for her stories?

   _____

   _____

5. What advice does Jane Yolen give to young writers?

   _____

   _____

   _____

6. When Jane Yolen is not writing books, what else does she like to do?

   _____

   _____

Introduction to Virtual Field Trips

Pack your bags and climb aboard! We're off to discover new places and fun-filled locations! On the following pages you will find field trips that span a variety of topics from trips to caves to trips to the zoo. Each trip has a key question or focus point that helps your students stay focused on their topics.

Key Questions and Statements

Trips Across America

What are the tools of the trade for someone who explores caves?

What kind of plant and animal life can be found in a cave?

How can the five senses help to explore something new?

What is the animal of the week and where does it live?

What animal is a good example of wildlife where you live?

What are the symbols of the state you've chosen?

Who are the workers in your community?

What decisions will you make to create your adventure?

How many animals can I find?

What important things or qualities in my life begin with the letters of my first name?

If I were going to design a room for the White House, what color would it be?

Key Questions and Statements *(cont.)*

Trips to the Animal Kingdom

Can you create an animal that has the features to survive anywhere in the world?

What animals live in Africa?

What is the most amazing animal in this exhibit and why?

What will I see on my virtual tour of the Ituri Forest?

What is the name and what are the colors of my favorite kind of butterfly?

How does a caterpillar become a butterfly?

What is the difference between a butterfly and a moth?

What are the physical characteristics and behaviors of crocodiles?

What characteristics of crocodilians helped them survive for 200 million years?

Trips Around the World

What is life like in the arctic?

What will I need to bring on a trip to the arctic?

What animals live in the arctic and how do they survive?

What was life like for kids in ancient Egypt?

What would my name look like if it were written in hieroglyphics?

What can I learn about the sphinx?

What is the same about life for students in Africa? What is different?

What happens in this story of a prince?

How do celebrations help keep traditions of a culture alive?

Curious Caves

Background

Have you ever been in an underground cave? What do you think of when you think about caves? Darkness? Bats? Water? Slime? Visit one of these virtual caves. What would you hope to find there?

Objectives

The student will identify helpful tools used in the hobby of caving (spelunking).

The student will examine key elements found in caves.

The student will explore features of the earth formed by nature.

The student will hypothesize how the five senses assist in exploration.

The Trip

Activity One: A Caver's Equipment

Key Question: What are the tools of the trade for someone who explores caves?

Activity Two: Life in a Sea Cave

Key Question: What kind of plant and animal life can be found in a cave?

Activity Three: The Five Senses Help Out

Key Question: How can the five senses help to explore something new?

Focus Web Site

Virtual Cave

http://www.goodearthgraphics.com/virtcave/index.html

Virtual Caves—Sea Caves

http://www.goodearthgraphics.com/virtcave/seacaves/seacaves.html

Google

http://www.google.com

(Keywords: virtual cave)

Name_____ Date _____

A Caver's Equipment

Key Question: What are the tools of the trade for someone who explores caves?

Directions: Every job, hobby, or craft has special tools or equipment that help the worker to get the job done. Look at the pictures on these pages, and read the introduction to the site.

1. What tools will help you in exploring a cave?

   _____

   _____

   _____

2. Draw a picture of what a caver might look like as he or she explores a dark cave.

Name_____ Date _____

Life in a Sea Cave

Key Question: What kind of plant and animal life can be found in a cave?

Directions: What does it take to live in a cave? There is very little light. It might be very wet. Read about life in a sea cave and look closely at the pictures.

1. Draw a picture of something that might be living in these caves.

Name_____ Date _____

The Five Senses Help Out

Key Question: How can the five senses help to explore something new?

Directions: Look at the cool things you would see in an underground cave. Then fill in the chart.

1. As a caver, you will need all five of your senses. What will each of your senses tell you?

Sense of touch: FINGERS	**Sense of hearing: EARS**
What will you touch in the cave?	**What will you hear in the cave?**
Sense of smell: NOSE	**Sense of taste: TONGUE**
What will you smell in the cave?	**What will you taste in the cave?**

Sense of sight: EYES
What will you see in the cave?

Wondrous Wildlife

Background

The United States is an enormous place with all different kinds of wildlife living in the different states. Some people like to travel in a recreational vehicle (RV) and watch for the various animals that poke their noses out to greet visitors.

Objectives

The student will identify a specific animal.

The student will write and illustrate a postcard of his/her own.

The student will identify the state bird, tree, and flower of another state.

The Trip

Activity One:

Key Question: What is the animal of the week and where does it live?

Activity Two: Home on the Range

Key Question: What animal is a good example of wildlife where you live?

Activity Three: Birds, Trees, and Flowers

Key Question: What are the symbols of the state you've chosen?

Focus Web Site

Focus Web Sites

Wildlife Postcard

http://www.postcardsfrom.com/h/scenic.html

(Note: You will need to a free subscription to receive the postcards of the week from this site.)

Postcard Gallery

http://www.postcardsfrom.com/t1/arcin.html

Google

http://www.google.com

(Keywords: postcards from America)

Name_____ Date _____

Wildlife Postcard

Key Question: What is the animal of the week and where does it live?

Directions: Read about the animal that is on this week's wildlife postcard. In the chart below, write sentences or draw pictures that tell a few facts you learned. Include where the animal lives, what state the postcard is from, what the animal eats, and a quick sketch of this animal.

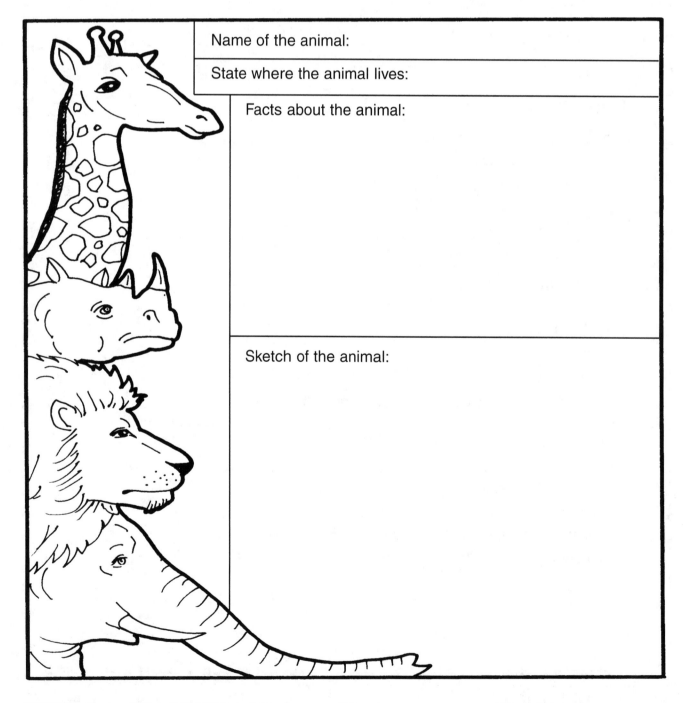

Name of the animal:
State where the animal lives:
Facts about the animal:
Sketch of the animal:

Name_____ Date _____

Home on the Range

Key Question: What animal is a good example of wildlife where you live?

Directions: Design a postcard that you would send from your home state showing an animal that lives there. Write any facts that you know about the animal on the back.

Front of postcard

Back of postcard

Name_____   Date _____

Birds, Trees, and Flowers

Key Question: What are the symbols of the state you've chosen?

Directions: Click on the link for the Postcard Gallery. Find the name of the state where you live or a state you would like to visit. Click on the link that says the week it was visited. Look at the postcard from that week. Does it look anything like where you live? Now click on the word "Stamps."

What is the state flower?_____

    Draw a picture of it in the box.

What is the state bird? _____

    Draw a picture of it in the box.

What is the state tree? _____

    Draw a picture of it in the box.

My Hometown

Background

There's no point in exploring the rest of the United States until you know what's in your own backyard. In this trip you'll stay within the borders of your own hometown and learn that truly, "There's no place like home!"

Objectives

The student will recall and record his/her own home address.

The student will identify the community helpers in his/her neighborhood.

The student will recall the number for emergencies and his/her own phone number.

The student will make decisions to determine the outcome of a story.

The student will practice identifying direction using a compass or compass rose.

The Trip

Activity One: Your Neighborhood

Key Question: Who are the workers in your community?

Activity Two: Design Your Own Adventure

Key Question: What decisions will you make to create your adventure?

Focus Web Site

Ben's Guide to U.S. Government for Kids

http://bensguide.gpo.gov/k-2/neighborhood/index.html

Design Your Own Adventure

http://www.jugband.org/kidstown/

(Click to visit Kids Town, then click on Go on a Journey.)

Google

http://www.google.com

(Keywords: kids government guide, kids online interactive stories)

Name_____ Date _____

Your Neighborhood

Key Question: Who are the workers in your community?

Directions: Your neighborhood has many people who are there to help you.

1. Where would the letter carrier take a letter addressed to you? Do you know your address? Write it on the lines below.

   _____

   _____

   _____

2. Who comes to help if you think there might be a fire at your house or nearby?

   _____

3. What are some things you can do to make sure a fire doesn't start?

   _____

   _____

   _____

4. In case of an emergency, you need to get to the phone right away. Do you know what number to call?

   _____ _____ _____

5. The person who answers the phone will ask you what your telephone number is.

   ____ ____ ____ — ____ ____ ____ ____

Name_____ Date _____

Design Your Own Adventure

Key Question: What decisions will you make to create your adventure?

Directions: Read each page of this story. Make choices along the way to create your own ending. Then fill in the circles below to tell what happened.

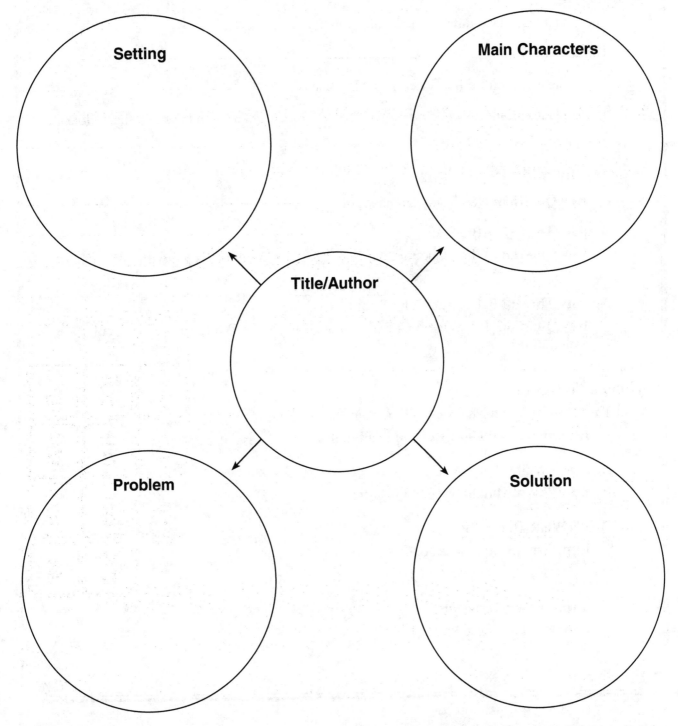

The White House

Background

The White House is an important part of American history. In this activity, students have the opportunity to meet some important White House residents—the pets! They will also learn more about a national landmark.

Objectives

The student will learn about a national landmark.

The student will count animals.

The student will create his or her own ABC books.

The student will identify his/her favorite colors and design a room based on that color.

The Trip

Activity One: Animals Everywhere!

    Key Question: How many animals can I find?

Activity Two: My ABC Book

    Key Question: What important things or qualities in my life begin with the letters of my first name?

Activity Three: My Favorite Color Room

    Key Question: If I were going to design a room for the White House, what color would it be?

Focus Web Site

The White House for Kids—Photo Album

    http://www.whitehouse.gov/kids/album/

Historical White House ABCs

    http://www.whitehouse.gov/kids/abc/

Spott's White House Tour

    http://www.whitehouse.gov/kids/tour/

Google

    http://www.google.com

(Keywords: white house kids)

Name_____ Date _____

Animals Everywhere!

Key Question: How many animals can I find?

Directions: Look at the first picture on the page. Click on the paw to see the other pictures.
Answer the questions below.

1. How many dogs live in the White House?

   _____

2. What are the names of the dogs?

   _____

3. How many cats live in the White House?

   _____

4. What is the name of the black cat?

   _____

5. Which animal that belongs to the president does not live in the White House?

   _____

6. Which animal is your favorite?

   _____

7. Draw a picture of your favorite animal in the box below.

Name_____ Date _____

My ABC Book

Key Question: What important things or qualities in my life begin with the letters of my first name?

Directions: Read Barney's ABC book. Barney uses different words that stand for people and qualities important to the White House. Write the letters of your first name in the boxes below. Then think of things or qualities important to you that begin with those letters. Write about them or draw pictures of them next to the letters.

_____	
_____	
_____	
_____	
_____	
_____	

Name_____ Date _____

My Favorite Color Room

Key Question: If I were going to design a room for the White House, what color would it be?

Directions: Look at the different rooms on the pages of Spotty's White House Tour. Which room do you like best, the green room, the red room, or the blue room? If you were going to design a room for the White House using your favorite color, what would it look like? Write the name of your favorite color and draw a picture below of what your room would look like.

My favorite color is _____

Beast or Fowl

Background

The parts of an animal's body are well suited to each animal's environment. For instance, a fish has gills and fins to survive in the water. A monkey has hand-like paws to use for gathering and eating food. If you could build a new animal from scratch, what features would you give him to be a super animal that could survive any environment? Mix and match the heads, bodies, and tails of these zoo animals!

Objectives

The student will identify various animal body parts and their functions.

The student will design an imaginary animal suited to a particular environment.

The student will use creative writing skills to describe an imaginary animal.

The Trip

Activity One: Survival of the Fittest

Key Question: Can you create an animal that has the features to survive anywhere in the world?

Activity Two: Animals of the World

Key Question: What animals live in Africa?

Teacher's Note: This lesson requires the FLASH plug-in.

Focus Web Site

Switcheroo Zoo

http://www.switcheroozoo.com/

KidsTown Zoo—Animals of Africa

http://www.jugband.org/kidstown/cgi-bin/kt.cgi?KEY=9200

Animals of Africa

http://readyed.com.au/Sites/zoo/africa.htm

Google

http://www.google.com

(Keywords: create own animal, zoo, Africa)

Name_____ Date _____

Survival of the Fittest

Key Question: Can you create an animal that has the features to survive anywhere in the world?

Directions: Combine different parts of real animals to make the perfect beast. What will you call him? What will this animal eat? How will this animal move? What kind of noise will it make? Who are its enemies? Who is afraid of this animal? Where does it live?

1. Draw a picture of your animal. Label the parts of its body.

2. Write a description or short story about your animal.

_____

_____

_____

_____

_____

Name_____ Date _____

Animals of the World

Key Question: What animals live in Africa?

Directions: Chances are, you will never see any of these African animals in your backyard! Look at the pictures of these beautiful animals. Choose two of your favorites and read more about them. In the spaces below, create two trading cards. The front of each card should be a color picture of the animal. The back of the card should give any information you think would be interesting to someone trading that card.

Animal Name: _____

Animal Name: _____

Cruise the Zoos!

Background

The zoo is home to reptiles, mammals, birds, and more. In this trip, students will explore zoos, visit some famous exhibits, and meet some amazing animals.

Objectives

The student will identify unusual animal characteristics.

The student will identify the animals and plants of an African jungle.

The Trip

Activity One: The Most Amazing Animals

Key Question: What is the most amazing animal in this exhibit and why?

Activity Two: Tour the Ituri Forest

Key Question: What will I see on my virtual tour of the Ituri Forest?

Focus Web Site

San Diego Zoo

http://www.sandiegozoo.org/

Animal Profiles for Kids

http://www.sandiegozoo.org/kids/animal_profiles.html

Ituri Forest

http://www.sandiegozoo.org/zoo/ex_ituri_forest.html

Google

http://www.google.com

(Keywords: San Diego Zoo, San Diego Zoo animal profiles, San Diego Zoo Ituri Forest)

Name_____ Date _____

The Most Amazing Animals

Key Question: What is the most amazing animal in this exhibit and why?

Directions: Select an animal to read about on the Animal Profiles page. Then answer the questions below.

1. What is the name of the animal or animals that you read about?

   _____

   _____

2. What kind of animal is it?

   _____

   _____

3. Why is this animal an amazing animal?

   _____

   _____

   _____

4. In the frame below, draw a picture of this amazing animal.

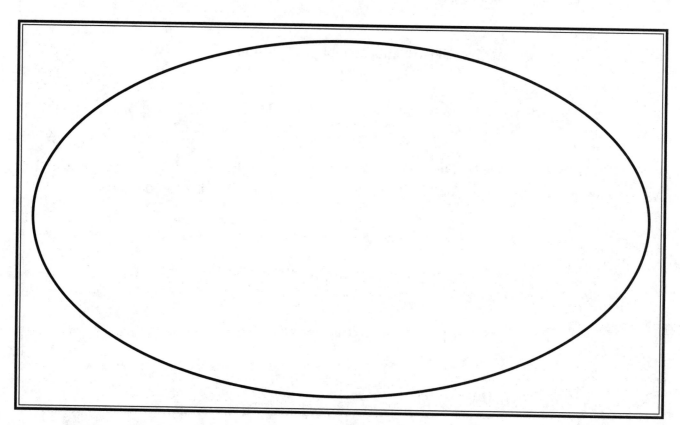

Name_____ Date _____

Tour the Ituri Forest

Key Question: What will I see on my virtual tour of the Ituri Forest?

Directions: Follow the links to take a virtual tour of the Ituri Forest. As you take the tour, answer the questions below.

1. What is the first animal you see on the page?

   _____

   _____

   _____

2. What is up in the trees?

   _____

   _____

3. What is splashing in the river?

   _____

4. Which animal would you most like to see? Why?

   _____

   _____

   _____

   _____

   _____

Beautiful Butterflies

Background

North America is home to a variety of butterflies of all different types and colors. In this activity, students will learn more about these beautiful insects.

Objectives

The student will identify different types of butterflies.

The student will describe the butterfly life cycle.

The student will identify how butterflies differ from moths.

The Trip

Activity One: My Favorite Butterfly

Key Question: What is the name and what are the colors of my favorite kind of butterfly?

Activity Two: Butterfly Life Cycle

Key Question: How does a caterpillar become a butterfly?

Activity Three: Butterfly or Moth?

Key Question: What is the difference between a butterfly and a moth?

Focus Web Sites

Butterflies and Moths of North America—Gallery

http://www.butterfliesandmoths.org/gallery

Butterfly Life Cycle

http://www.shrewsbury-ma.gov/schools/beal/curriculum/butterfly/cycle/index.htm

Moth or Butterfly?

http://www.shrewsbury-ma.gov/schools/beal/curriculum/butterfly/mothorbutterfly.html

Google

http://www.google.com

Keywords: butterflies, butterfly life cycle, "moth or butterfly")

Page 119 answers: 1. butterfly, 2. moth, 3. moth, 4. butterfly, 5. moth.

Name_____ Date _____

My Favorite Butterfly

Key Question: What is the name and what are the colors of my favorite kind of butterfly?

Directions: Look at the different butterflies on this page. Click on a little picture to see a bigger picture.

1. Which butterfly do you like best? Write its name on the line below.

_____

2. Use crayons or colored pencils to show what your favorite butterfly looks like.

Name_____ Date _____

Butterfly Life Cycle

Key Question: How does a caterpillar become a butterfly?

Directions: Click on the butterfly pictures to see the butterfly life cycle. Write the names of the stages and draw pictures of them below.

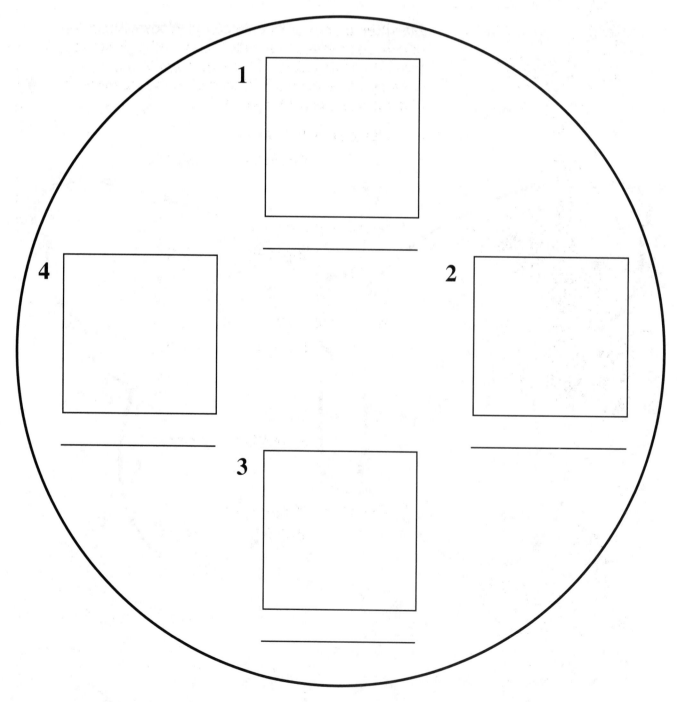

Name_____ Date _____

Butterfly or Moth?

Key Question: What is the difference between a butterfly and a moth?

Directions: Look at the Web page to learn about the differences between butterflies and moths. Then read the statements below. If the statement is about a butterfly, circle the word "Butterfly." If the statement is about a moth, circle the word "Moth."

1. Has a smooth body—

   Butterfly   **Moth**

2. Grows in a cocoon—

   Butterfly   **Moth**

3. Is active at night—

   Butterfly   **Moth**

4. Has upright wings—

   Butterfly   **Moth**

5. Has dull-colored wings—

   Butterfly   **Moth**

Ancient Reptiles

Background

Crocodiles and alligators, members of the crocodilian species, are less famous than their popular relatives, the dinosaurs. The crocodile's ancestors shared the land and sea with dinosaurs and flying reptiles more than 200 million years ago. Their unique combination of physical and behavioral characteristics allowed the 23 species of crocodilians to outlive their dinosaur cousins by 65 million years. In this trip, students will study the unusual characteristics of crocodiles, learn about different species, and discover the special qualities responsible for their amazing survival.

Objectives

The student will gather information about crocodilians from Web resources.

The student will identify the physical characteristics and behaviors of crocodilians.

The student will organize and categorize information in a table.

The student will identify the characteristics and behaviors responsible for the survival of the crocodilian species.

The Trip

Activity One: Incredible Crocodiles

Key Question: What are the physical characteristics and behaviors of crocodiles?

Activity Two: Survivor!

Key Question: What characteristics of crocodilians helped them survive for 200 million years?

Teacher's Note: This lesson requires the FLASH plug-in.

Focus Web Site

The Clickable Croc

http://www.pbs.org/wgbh/nova/crocs/clickable/

Crocodiles—Outlasting the Dinosaurs

http://www.pbs.org/wgbh/nova/crocs/dinosaurs/

Google

http://www.google.com

(Keywords: crocodiles, crocodiles outlasting dinosaurs)

Name_____ Date _____

Incredible Crocodiles

Key Question: What are the physical characteristics and behaviors of crocodiles?

Directions: Summarize and enter the most important facts about the crocodile in the table. Next, use the information you collected to make a guess about how the crocodile has survived for millions of years. When finished, write down your crocodile survival ideas in the box at the bottom of the page.

Body Part or Word	Important Facts

My Ideas About How the Crocodile Survived

Name_____ Date _____

Survivor!

Key Question: What characteristics of crocodilians helped them survive for 200 million years?

Directions: Read the web page about crocodiles outlasting the dinosaurs. Write down 10 reasons discussed in the interview that explain why crocodiles survive. Decide if the reason is a physical characteristic or a behavior. In the Physical Characteristic or Behavior column, write "P" for physical and "B" for behavior. When finished, look at your ideas in the box from the previous activity about how crocodiles survived. Compare your ideas with the information from the Web sites. See if you were able to figure out how the crocodiles outlasted the dinosaurs!

	Reason for Survival	**Physical Characteristic or Behavior?**
1.		
2.		
3.		
4.		
5.		
6.		
7.		
8.		
9.		
10.		

Arctic Adventure

Background

The Arctic Circle is one of the coldest places on earth, yet it is full of life and adventure. Learn more about this amazing continent, figure out what to bring along on a trip to the arctic, and see how animals have adapted to life there.

Objectives

The student will learn about life in the arctic.

The student will learn about arctic animals.

The student will identify attributes that help animals survive in the arctic.

The Trip

Activity One: Life in the Arctic
   Key Question: What is life like in the arctic?

Activity Two: You'll Need a Jacket
   Key Question: What will I need to bring on a trip to the arctic?

Activity Three: Arctic Adaptations
   Key Question: What animals live in the arctic and how do they survive?

Focus Web Site

Enchanted Learning—Arctic Animals
   http://www.enchantedlearning.com/coloring/arcticanimals.shtml

Virtual Tour--Antarctica
   http://astro.uchicago.edu/cara/vtour/

Artic Adaptations
   http://www.seaworld.org/fun-zone/fun-guides/arctic/arctic-adaptations.htm

Google
   http://www.google.com
(Keywords: arctic animals, artic animals adaptation)

Name_____ Date _____

Life in the Arctic

Key Question: What is life like in the arctic?

Directions: Learn more about what the arctic is like and answer the questions below.

1. When does the arctic have long periods of light?

   _____

   _____

2. Which arctic zone supports more life?

   _____

   _____

3. What kind of animals hibernate?

   _____

   _____

4. When do animals migrate?

   _____

   _____

Look at the pictures of animals that live in the arctic. Draw your favorite below.

Name_____ Date _____

You'll Need a Jacket

Key Question: What will I need to bring on a trip to the arctic?

Directions: Complete the activities below.

1. After you take your virtual trip of the artic, think about what would you need to bring. Draw pictures of these items in the box below.

2. On the lines below, write items you would **NOT** need to bring.

_____

_____

_____

_____

Name_____ Date _____

Arctic Adaptations

Key Question: What animals live in the arctic and how do they survive?

Directions: Read about how different animals in the arctic adapt to the cold. Answer the questions below.

1. How does the polar bear adapt to the cold?

    _____

    _____

    _____

2. How do beluga whales, walruses, and seals adapt to the cold?

    _____

    _____

    _____

3. How does the arctic fox adapt to the cold?

    _____

    _____

    _____

4. What do you think is the best way to adapt to the cold? Why?

    _____

    _____

    _____

Life in Ancient Egypt

Background

Ancient Egypt was a rich culture that is still studied today. In this trip, students will learn about the sphinx, imagine their daily lives if they lived in ancient Egypt, and write their names in hieroglyphics.

Objectives

The student will learn about daily life in ancient Egypt.

The student will write their names in hieroglyphics.

The student will learn about the sphinx.

The Trip

Activity One: If I Lived in Ancient Egypt

    Key Question: What was life like for kids in ancient Egypt?

Activity Two: My Name in Hieroglyphics

    Key Question: What would my name look like if it were written in hieroglyphics?

Activity Three: The Sphinx

    Key Question: What can I learn about the sphinx?

Focus Web Site

Ancient Egyptian Life

    http://www.ancientegypt.co.uk/life/home.html

Make Your Own Cartouche

    http://www.harcourtschool.com/activity/cartouche/cartouche.html

Guardian's Sphinx

    http://www.guardians.net/egypt/sphinx/

Google

    http://www.google.com

(Keywords: Ancient Egyptian life, make own cartouche, sphinx)

Name_____ Date _____

If I Lived in Ancient Egypt

Key Question: What was life like for kids in ancient Egypt?

Directions: Read about daily life in ancient Egypt. Then write a story about what your life would be like if you lived in ancient Egypt. What would you wear? Would you go to school? What would you eat?

If I lived in ancient Egypt...

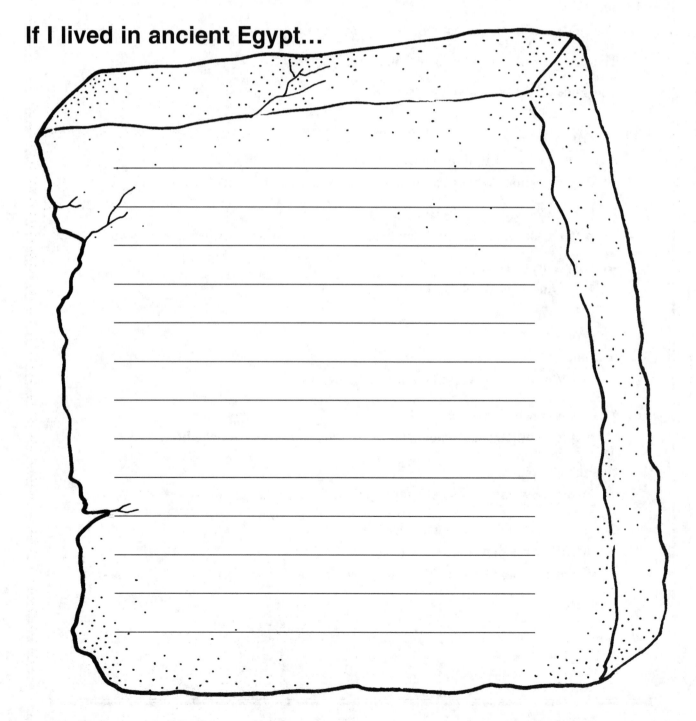

Name_____ Date _____

My Name in Hieroglyphics

Key Question: What would my name look like if it were written in hieroglyphics?

Directions: Type your name in the box and press **Enter** to see what your name would look like in hieroglyphics.

My name is: _____

Here is what my name would look like in hieroglyphics.

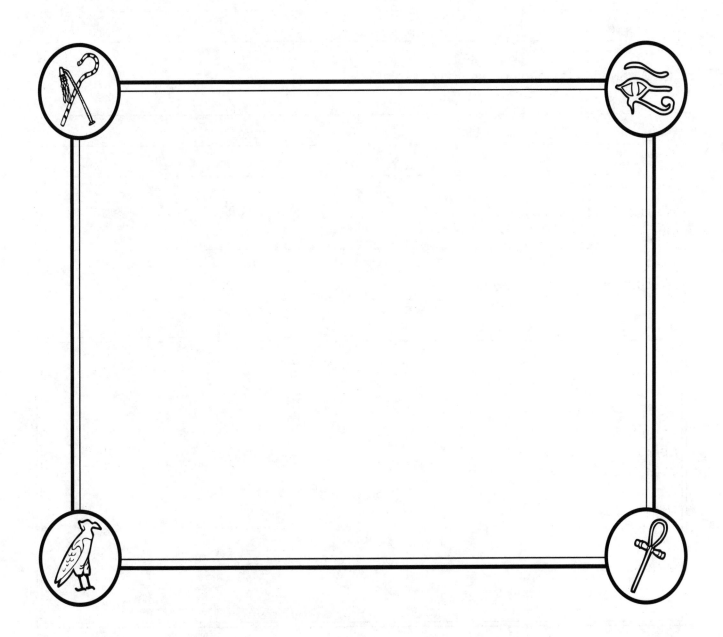

Name_____ Date _____

The Sphinx

Key Question: What can I learn about the sphinx?

Directions: The sphinx is a well-known symbol of ancient Egypt. The most famous sphinx is the sphinx found in Giza. Read the Web page to learn more about the sphinx, then answer the questions and draw the sphinx below.

1. What does the head of the sphinx look like?

   _____

   _____

   _____

2. What does the body of the sphinx look like?

   _____

   _____

   _____

3. How long is the sphinx?

   _____

4. Draw the sphinx in the box below.

Children of Africa

Background

On this continent far away, boys and girls just like you wake up and start their days. But what they do, what they eat, and where they go are very different from the things you do each day. Meet Femi, and learn what life is like for kids in Africa!

Objectives

The student will identify the similarities and differences of life in different countries.

The student will listen to a native folk tale and summarize the story in pictures.

The student will recognize that different cultures have their own traditions.

The Trip

Activity One: Student Life in Uganda

Key Question: What is the same about life for students in Africa? What is different?

Activity Two: A Swahili Folk Tale

Key Question: What happens in this story of a prince?

Activity Three: Hunting for Food

Key Question: How do celebrations help keep traditions of a culture alive?

Focus Web Site

PBS: Africa for Kids—Student Life in Uganda
http://pbskids.org/africa/myworld/mengo.html

PBS: Africa for Kids—Swahili Folk Tale
http://pbskids.org/africa/tale/index.html

PBS: Africa For Kids—Make a Mask
http://pbskids.org/africa/mask/index.html

Google
http://www.google.com

(Keywords: Africa for kids, student life Uganda, Swahili folk tale, Dogon mask)

Name_____ Date _____

Student Life in Uganda

Key Question: What is the same about life for students in Africa? What is different?

Directions: Students in the country of Uganda work very hard at their schoolwork. Some students from the United States have already asked them questions. What can you find out about their lives? See if you can find the answers to these questions, and then think about what questions you would like to ask these kids.

1. How do these students get to school?

    _____

2. What is one thing that is the same about your school and theirs?

    _____

    _____

    _____

3. What time do these students go to school in the morning?

    _____

4. What time do they go home?

    _____

5. What questions would you like to ask these kids?

    _____

    _____

    _____

6. Write an e-mail to the students at Kampala.

    _____

    _____

    _____

Name_____ Date _____

A Swahili Folk Tale

Key Question: What happens in this story of a prince?

Directions: Every culture has its own favorite folk tales and stories. Here is one about a prince that needed help on a journey. You can read the story yourself, or click on the speaker to have it read to you. (The *RealAudio Player* is needed to hear this story.)

Write the letter of each correct answer to the left of the question.

___ Who does the prince meet first on his journey?

___ What task are these creatures able to help the prince do?

___ Who does the prince meet next?

___ What task are these creatures able to help the prince do?p

___ Who does the prince meet next?

___ What task are these creatures able to help the prince do?

a. Djinns

b. crickets

c. birds

d. sort seeds

e. cut down a tree

f. find the princess

g. find his brothers

Draw a picture to show the events of the story in the correct order.

Beginning   Middle   End

Name_____ Date _____

Hunting for Food

Key Question: How do celebrations help keep traditions of a culture alive?

Directions: In America, we keep some of our traditions alive through celebrations. Thanksgiving is one of those celebrations. In Africa, the tradition of hunting for food is kept alive through dance. The Dogon people celebrate the hunt by wearing masks and acting out the chase of the hunter and rabbit. You can watch the Dogon dance, and then try acting out the hunt on the playground yourselves.

1. Cut out and color the pattern below and on the next page to make a mask of the hunter or the rabbit. Other masks can be found on the Africa for Kids Web site.

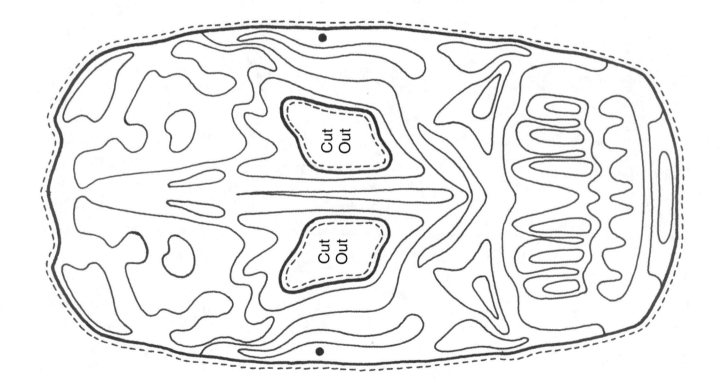

Mask Pattern

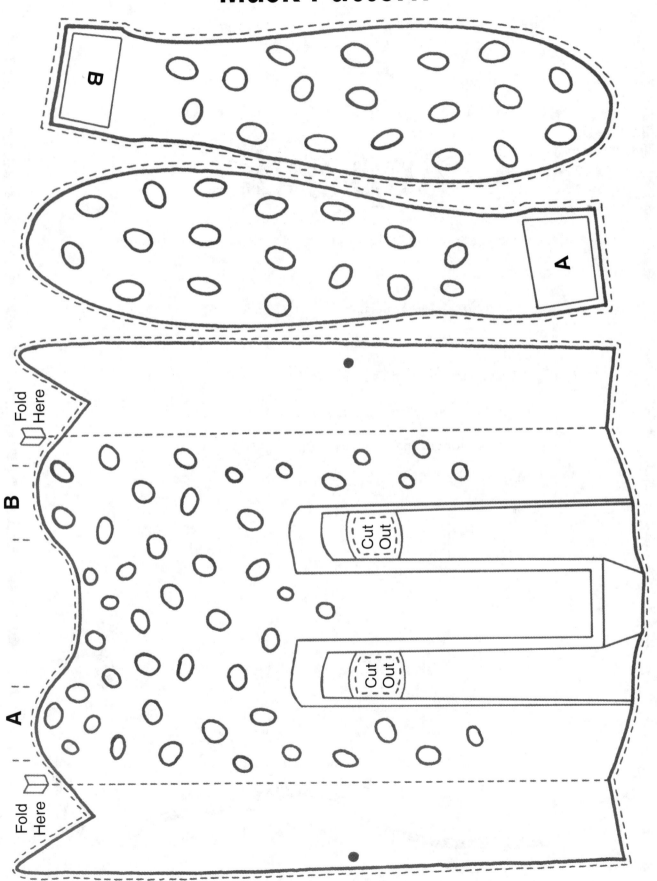

Appendix

Creating Your Own Web Hunts & Virtual Field Trips

When you're ready to start creating your own Web hunts and virtual field trips, there are a few things you'll want to keep in mind to make the process run smoothly.

1. Always start with the curriculum first.

    Whether you're building a Web hunt or a virtual field trip, you'll want to be sure that you start with the curriculum as your focus. Being clear about your learning objectives is the best way to create a sound educational tool.

2. Make decisions about what you're going to search for BEFORE you start searching.

    Using search engines can be a very frustrating process. It is easy to get lost or to travel too far down a "side street" that leads nowhere. Become familiar with a few of the many search engines and Web site collections before you begin a serious or time-intensive search. One of the best things you can do is to visit the "Help" sections of the search engine sites. They provide valuable information about how to use each specific search engine.

3. Collect more sites than you think you'll need.

    Plan on collecting about two times as many sites as you're planning to use in your actual activity. That way you'll have sites to fall back on if they go down either temporarily or permanently. It's also nice to have extras because then you'll have lots of options, and you can pick the best sites to match your objectives.

4. Examine the sites from a student's perspective.

    One of the most important things to consider when evaluating Web sites for student use is readability. Is the content of the site on a reading level that matches your students' needs? Look for other things, too, like excess information, over abundance of "eye candy" (unnecessary graphics), confusing layouts, or inappropriate advertising.

5. Construct activity pages to go along with each activity.

    Remember that your students are going online to collect or review information (Web hunts) or to explore and get to know information (virtual field trips). Either way, they'll need a place to take notes, collect data, or construct learning, so give them some organizational tools to help them stay on task!

Building Hunts and Trips Work Sheet

Content Area: _____   **Grade Level:** _____

Learning objectives/benchmarks I want to support:

1. _____
2. _____
3. _____

Search words to use when searching for sites:

Web Site Collection

URL	Quick Description
_____	_____
_____	_____
_____	_____
_____	_____
_____	_____
_____	_____
_____	_____

Building Hunts and Trips Work Sheet *(cont.)*

Now that I've collected all the sites I think I might use, it's time to narrow down my focus to just a few of the sites and to build activities to go along with them. The best way to construct an activity is to focus on what my students can actively do by either collecting data or using data in another activity. It is helpful to decide if the site is best for **information collection (IC)** or for an **activity (A)**.

Web site   **IC/A**

_____   _____

What can my kids DO on this site?

    1. _____

    2. _____

Web site   **IC/A**

_____   _____

What can my kids DO on this site?

    1. _____

    2. _____

Web site   **IC/A**

_____   _____

What can my kids DO on this site?

    1. _____

    2. _____

Web site   **IC/A**

_____   _____

What can my kids DO on this site?

    1. _____

    2. _____

Our Internet Rules

The Internet is a special tool that can help me learn, communicate and solve problems. Before I can use the Internet at my school, there are some promises that I need to make to my teacher, my classmates, my parents and myself. These promises are made to help keep me safe and to make my time on the Internet fun, interesting and educational.

When I use the Internet, I promise to . . .

. . . treat the people I "meet" on the Internet and the machines I use with respect.

. . . act as a representative of my school, showing everyone that I can act responsibly.

. . . tell my teacher or another adult when I see or my group sees something which is inappropriate or makes me feel uncomfortable.

. . . follow all of the instructions my teacher gives and stay only in the areas he/she suggests to me.

. . . actively use the information I find on the Internet in my learning (projects, reports, discussions).

. . . use the Internet as a learning tool to help me discover my world. I should know WHY I'm using the Internet for a certain task.

. . . share the activities I do on the Internet at home. It's important to let Mom and Dad know what I'm doing on the Internet and why I'm there.

. . . be aware that there are consequences for choosing not to follow the Internet rules.

I understand that my teacher knows how to keep me safe on the Internet, so it's important for me to follow directions. I understand that there are some things on the Internet that are not meant for children. If I find anything on the Internet that makes me feel uncomfortable, I know it's important to share that with my teacher right away.

Student Signature:_____   Teacher Signature: _____

Parent Signature:_____   Principal Signature: _____

© 1997 Internet Mentors Field Guide, Orange County Public Schools
Reprinted with permission from the author, Deirdre Kelly dkelly@magicnet.net

We're Responsible Users!

When I use the Internet, I promise to…

. . . treat the people I "meet" on the Internet and the machines I use with respect.

. . . act as a representative of my school, showing everyone that I can act responsibly.

. . . tell my teacher or another adult when I see or my group sees something which is inappropriate or makes me feel uncomfortable.

. . . follow all of the instructions my teacher gives and stay only in the areas he/she suggests to me.

. . . actively use the information I find on the Internet in my learning (projects, reports, discussions).

. . . use the Internet as a learning tool to help me discover my world. I should know WHY I'm using the Internet for a certain task.

. . . share the activities I do on the Internet at home. It's important to let Mom and Dad know what I'm doing on the Internet and why I'm there.

. . . be aware that there are consequences for choosing not to follow the Internet rules.

© 1997 Internet Mentors Field Guide, Orange County Public Schools
Reprinted with permission from the author, Deirdre Kelly dkelly@magicnet.net

Internet Research Road Map

I need to find...   (Be specific!)

My plan for finding it is...

☐ I have permission to use search engines for the information I need to find. I'm going to run searches on these words:

☐ I don't have permission to use search engines, but my teacher suggested that I research on these Web sites.

Site(s) I can visit: 1. _____

2. _____

Time I started: _____ Time I'm allowed online: _____ Time stopped: _____

The results of my search...(Be sure to take notes on what you find! Use the back of this page too!)

Directions for Getting Graphics Off the Internet

Before we get started, here's a word or two about permissions:

Most online images/graphics are copyright protected and, although educational use is often taken for granted, you must contact the Webmaster to get permission to use any images obtained from a Web site.

How to Get Permission

Getting permission from the site creator might sound daunting, but it is usually a very simple task. On most Web sites there is an e-mail link to the Webmaster. Simply use that link to send an e-mail. Be sure to introduce yourself and explain that you wish to use the image/graphic for educational use. Tell exactly how you want to use the graphic (in class, a handout, a multimedia presentation, etc.). If you give all the information right up front, you'll save yourself some time.

Graphic Grabs

Now that you have permission, let's go to it. Here's how to get a graphic/image off the Internet so that you can insert it into a document, save it as a graphics file, etc.

1. Put your cursor directly on top of the graphic or image you wish to capture.

2. Click and hold down your mouse button (use the right mouse button on PC compatibles) until a menu of options appears.

3. Select the option "Save Image As."

4. A "Save As" window will appear. Now this task is just like saving any other document or file. Direct the "Save As" window to the location where you wish to store the graphic and hit "Save." TIP: It's helpful to have a file called "Graphics" just for images and graphics.

5. You're finished!

When you're ready to use this graphic, just go to your word processing program, open the document you want to use (or create a new one), and use your usual procedure for inserting a graphic/clip art!

One outstanding use for this procedure is to capture a variety of really diverse and interesting graphics and then use them as journal starters or writing response exercises. Put the graphic at the top of a blank page and have your students write their responses to it on the bottom half.

Glossary

Data Collection

Data collection refers to the collection of information. Data collection takes many forms – getting answers to a survey, taking notes during class, and even writing a shopping list while you stand in front of your half-empty refrigerator! In this book data collection usually refers to the gathering of information or taking notes from a Web site.

Eye Candy

If you've ever been to a Web site where there's just too much material, you are looking at eye candy. Dancing frogs and scrolling messages are examples. There's nothing really (technically) wrong with eye candy, other than it may be in bad taste and that it can slow the page down a bit. It's important to realize that the extraneous information makes it very easy for kids to get distracted or even to go clicking off in other directions.

Graphic Organizer

A graphic organizer is a paper divided up into sections to hold information (usually for some kind of data collection). There are many customized graphic organizers in the pages of this book.

Online

When something is referred to as an "online" activity, it means that you need to be on the Internet while you're completing the activity.

Offline

Offline activities are those activities that do not require the Internet.

Readability

The readability of a Web site is similar to the readability of a book. It refers to the grade level of the text. What ages or grades can read the Web site? This is an important question to ask yourself when you're creating your own hunts and trips.

Search Engines

Search engines are online tools used to help locate online information. They are similar to an encyclopedic index or a phone book, except there's much more information to sort through.

URL

A uniform resource locator (URL) is commonly referred to as a Web site address.

Virtual Field Trip

An online activity based on a location of some kind is a virtual field trip.

Web Hunt

An online activity based on the collection of information is a web hunt.